Adventure Racing Activities for Fun and Fitness

Dan DeJager

Cathrine Himberg

Human Kinetics

Library of Congress Cataloging-in-Publication Data

DeJager, Dan.
  Adventure racing activities for fun and fitness / Dan DeJager, Cathrine Himberg.
    p. cm.
  Includes bibliographical references.
  ISBN-13: 978-0-7360-6924-3 (soft cover)
  ISBN-10: 0-7360-6924-0 (soft cover)
  1. Adventure racing. I. Himberg, Cathrine, 1965- II. Title.
GV1038.D45 2008
796.5--dc22

                    2007050412

ISBN-10: 0-7360-6924-0
ISBN-13: 978-0-7360-6924-3

The Web addresses cited in this text were current as of November 2007, unless otherwise noted.

Acquisitions Editor: Scott Wikgren; **Developmental Editor:** Anne Hall; **Assistant Editor:** Cory Weber; **Copyeditor:** John Wentworth; **Proofreader:** Patrick Connolly; **Permission Manager:** Carly Breeding; **Graphic Designer:** Joe Buck; **Graphic Artist:** Tara Welsch; **Cover Designer:** Keith Blomberg; **Photographers (cover):** John Roussell and Dan DeJager; **Photographers (interior):** John Roussell and Dan DeJager, unless otherwise noted; **Photo Asset Manager:** Laura Fitch; **Visual Production Assistant:** Joyce Brumfield; **Photo Office Assistant:** Jason Allen; **Art Manager:** Kelly Hendren; **Associate Art Manager/Illustrator:** Alan L. Wilborn; **Printer:** United Graphics

Printed in the United States of America   10 9 8 7 6 5 4 3 2 1

Human Kinetics
Web site: www.HumanKinetics.com

United States: Human Kinetics
P.O. Box 5076
Champaign, IL 61825-5076
800-747-4457
e-mail: humank@hkusa.com

Canada: Human Kinetics
475 Devonshire Road Unit 100
Windsor, ON N8Y 2L5
800-465-7301 (in Canada only)
e-mail: info@hkcanada.com

Europe: Human Kinetics
107 Bradford Road
Stanningley
Leeds LS28 6AT, United Kingdom
+44 (0) 113 255 5665
e-mail: hk@hkeurope.com

Australia: Human Kinetics
57A Price Avenue
Lower Mitcham, South Australia 5062
08 8372 0999
e-mail: info@hkaustralia.com

New Zealand: Human Kinetics
Division of Sports Distributors NZ Ltd.
P.O. Box 300 226 Albany
North Shore City
Auckland
0064 9 448 1207
e-mail: info@humankinetics.co.nz

To my parents, my brother, and my sister. It was with you that I first learned the importance of cooperation and teamwork. To my wife, Kristen, for your support in this adventure race we call life.

—Dan DeJager

To all the REAL teachers (www.supportREALteachers.org) who are doing their best every day to help kids develop the skills, knowledge, and desire they need to be active for life. You make a difference!

—Cathrine Himberg

Contents

Activity Finder

OBSTACLES	PAGE	EQUIPMENT NEEDED	SUITABLE FOR INDOORS	JUDGE REQUIRED	ACCEPTABLE FOR YOUNGER STUDENTS (K-3)
Fitness					
Bear Crawl	44		X		X
Crab Crawl	44		X		X
Crunches	45	X	X		X
Dips	45	X	X		
Flutter Kicks	46		X		X
Cross Countries	46		X		X
Horizontal Arm Rotations	47		X		X
Jumping Jacks	47		X		X
Jump Rope	48	X	X		X
Kick Backs	48		X		
Knee Tappers	49		X		
Lunges	49		X		X
Lunge Walk	50		X		X
Mountain Climbers	50		X		
Outside Leg Lifts	51		X		
Pop-Ups	51		X		
Push-Ups	52		X		X
Sit-Ups	52	X	X		
Squats	53		X		X
Star Jumps	53		X		
Vertical Arm Rotations	54		X		X
Wall Sit	54	X	X		

OBSTACLES	PAGE	EQUIPMENT NEEDED	SUITABLE FOR INDOORS	JUDGE REQUIRED	ACCEPTABLE FOR YOUNGER STUDENTS (K-3)
Skill					
Disc Throw	56	X	X	X	X
Football Throwing	56	X	X	X	
Soccer Passing	56	X	X	X	X
Line Dancing	56		X	X	
Social and Ballroom Dancing	57		X	X	
Golf Pitching	57	X		X	
Tennis Racket Control	57	X	X	X	
Volleyball Bumping	57	X	X	X	
Basketball Dribbling and Passing	58	X	X	X	X
Problem Solving and Team Building					
Blind Man's Bridge	59	X		X	X
Instruction Board	60	X	X	X	X
Lava River	61	X		X	
Lily Pad Leap	62	X		X	X
Ring of Power	63	X		X	

Preface

I carried my teammate's mountain bike as well as my own as I trudged through the thick sand toward the transition area. I looked back and saw Eli, one of my teammates, pushing Carrie, our third teammate, on her mountain bike toward me. Carrie was slumped forward in the seat, unable to help progress the team forward. Behind my two teammates I saw another team. One of the members was carrying a couple of bikes, while his teammate pushed a bike with one hand and carried a woman (his third teammate) slung over his shoulder with the other. All of this was part of the rules for this section of the race. One member of the team was unconscious, one bike could be only pushed, not ridden, and another bike had to be carried.

This was a challenge called "Disaster Scenario"—one of the many challenges our team faced that day. We had already biked several miles, kayaked a few miles on a lake, and completed many other small obstacles. We still had several more miles to run, and several more challenges to overcome, including getting the entire team over a 12-foot (3.7 m) wall, before we could cross the finish line. Some workouts are boring. This one was anything but. Before we were finished I knew this wouldn't be my last adventure race.

This experience was unlike anything I had done before. I was thankful that a stranger at my gym had told me about the event, and I wanted to spread the news as well. I wanted to share the idea of adventure racing with my physical education classes, to put together an adventure race for them, but I knew there would be challenges. My school doesn't have a set of mountain bikes or anywhere for students to ride them. We don't have kayaks, and even if we did we have no water nearby to put them on. No bikes, no kayaks, no place to ride, no place to float . . . there was no other choice but to exclude bikes and kayaks from the race. I would have to replace them with other obstacles for students to complete. But I was resolute that changing obstacles would not change the spirit of the adventure race. Students would still complete a cooperative obstacle racing experience (CORE), but it would be an adventure race customized for physical education. This race would employ the core ideas of adventure racing (all the good stuff that made me love it) without the fancy equipment or the risk.

That first race was successful. Students seemed to like adventure racing far more than running a mile the traditional way, and they were working on teamwork skills at the same time. It wasn't long before other physical education teachers in my department started trying adventure races with their classes as well. Soon we had an entire adventure racing unit, which many students claim is their favorite of the year.

Remembering the stranger who had shared the sport of adventure racing with me, I presented some ideas at a few state physical education conferences, and at a national conference. I wanted other physical education teachers to know about adventure racing. Things developed and progressed, and now, with the help of my friend and colleague Cathrine Himberg, we have this book. I hope it motivates you in the same way I was motivated by my first adventure race.

—Dan DeJager

Getting students excited about moving and helping them develop lifelong exercise habits are great challenges for physical education teachers. Now more than ever there's an urgency in our mission for physical education. We have been charged with the responsibility to help curb the rise in childhood obesity by helping kids develop the skills, knowledge, and dispositions needed to be active now and for the rest of their lives. When teachers like Dan create activities that motivate kids to exercise and learn, it becomes easier to plan the types of lessons and units that do it all: keep kids moving in class, work on health-related fitness, and teach skills and concepts that students need in order to be active now and in the future. (In other words, lessons that address the national standards for physical education and help children become physically educated people.)

I was excited when Dan asked me to help him write this book, and to be able to write my sections with integrity, I had to try out adventure racing CORE and see for myself how the ideas worked with kids. For six semesters my secondary methods teacher preparation course has included adventure racing CORE. My university students have taught the students in our local alternative education classes (7th through 12th grade) numerous lessons using the adventure racing CORE program. And I'm sold! The effort that the junior high and high school kids put into each race has amazed me. Their diligence in completing the race obstacles, their responsible behaviors, and their smiling faces have shocked their regular teachers. Meanwhile, my university students are excited about an alternative method to boost activity levels when they teach skills and concepts. And that's how I see the adventure racing CORE program—as a new and exciting alternative method of delivering our content. You can teach skills and concepts and promote responsibility all in one setup. You can keep kids active in class and teach them what they need to know to be active now and for the rest of their lives—all while using a format that keeps them motivated and having fun!

Enjoyment is key to fostering healthy activity habits. We tend to do the things we *like* to do. However, having fun is not a stand-alone goal for physical education; any babysitter can have fun with kids while keeping them moving. But having fun while learning lifetime skills, meaningful concepts, and responsibility—all focused on the NASPE standards—can be done. You might find, as we have, that adventure racing CORE is a great way to accomplish that goal.

—Cathrine Himberg

Acknowledgments

We would like to express our gratitude to the people who have contributed to this book in a variety of ways.

Our appreciation goes to John Roussell, professor in the communication design department at California State University at Chico, who designed and developed most of the pictures for the book. Thanks for providing us with illustrative and meaningful visuals to make our ideas clear to the readers.

We are grateful to the amazing team at Human Kinetics. Scott Wikgren, without your excitement about the idea in the first place, there would be no book. Anne Hall, our developmental editor, your feedback was excellent and helped guide us through the toughest part of writing. Thanks to the editorial, production, and marketing staff—we feel privileged to have had your professional, capable hands involved in this project.

To Dan's colleagues in the physical education department at Churchill Middle School in Sacramento—Jeff Darrow, Lisa Ezekiel, Joel Lorenzo, Breanna Parker, Jamie Jungk, and Pam McKinney. Thank you for being excited, supportive, and helpful when trying new adventure racing ideas. Thanks also to all the students who participated in the many races and helped Dan refine his ideas for adventure racing CORE.

Thanks to alternative education teachers Matt McGuire and Lori Castaldo as well as the students at the Academy for Change in Chico for participating in so many adventure racing CORE lessons, for providing feedback, and for being excellent models for our pictures. And thanks to the students in the Physical Education Teacher Education (PETE) program at CSU-Chico (six semesters' worth of KINE 484 students) for teaching those lessons and sharing their ideas.

To our spouses, Kristen and John, thanks for your thoughts and support throughout the writing of this book.

And finally, thanks to the many physical education teachers who were willing to try adventure racing CORE in their classes and share their thoughts with us.

1
The Little Race That Eats Ironmen for Breakfast

Adventure racing is an exciting sport that's growing in popularity. A sport unlike any other, it might be compared to an adventurous and team-oriented triathlon. In adventure racing physical training is important, but the fittest participants don't always win. Races can take place in cities, in schools, or in the middle of nowhere. In this chapter we give a brief background on adventure racing and some of the history behind the sport. We also discuss how adventure racing can be modified to suit physical education classes, without fancy equipment or facilities.

Adventure races can take place in a variety of settings. In this one, racers run in teams through a local park.

BACKGROUND AND HISTORY

Associated Press

Adventure races were made popular in the United States by the Eco-Challenge, an extreme expedition race created by Mark Burnett, who also produced the popular reality show *Survivor*. A former section commander in the British Army Parachute Regiment, Burnett moved to the United States, where his first job was working in Beverly Hills as a nanny. In 1991, Burnett read an article about an adventure competition called the Raid Gauloises.

Mark Burnett, famous for developing reality shows such as *Survivor* and *The Apprentice*, has done much to promote adventure racing as a high-profile sport.

Gerard Fusil, the French coordinator of the Raid Gauloises, is often considered the godfather of adventure racing. The Raid took place in a different exotic location every year. Five-person teams traveled several hundred miles in races that lasted up to two weeks. Teams that participated in the expedition race had to carry their own food, water, and any gear they needed. The race was similar to races Burnett knew of that were held in New Zealand.

A group of modestly talented individuals who are team players will accomplish far more than an assortment of geniuses thinking only of themselves. My expedition racing taught me that. I can think of no greater test of human dynamics than a team racing in an Eco-Challenge and forced to spend every minute of every day together for two weeks.

Mark Burnett, producer of Eco-Challenge, from his book *Dare to Succeed.*

Mark Burnett decided to do his own expedition race called the Eco-Challenge. He gathered sponsors and raced the Raid himself so he would know how racers felt. To lure in racers he ran ads in *Triathlete* magazine, claiming that "This Little Race Eats Ironmen for Breakfast." Together with his management team, Burnett produced the Eco-Challenge, which was widely televised to viewers who had never seen anything like it before (Burnett, 2001). As more and more Eco-Challenges were produced, adventure racing gained popularity.

Because of the popularity of the Eco-Challenge, adventure races grew in numbers, each with its own spin. Some were only a few hours long, whereas others took days to complete. Some took place in cities, and others in wild, exotic places. The popularity of the sport continued to rise. In 2001, at a race in Folsom, California, over 1,000 competitors participated (Murphy and McEntegart, 2001). In 2007,

The personal challenges inherent in adventure racing lend themselves to memorable experiences for both participants and spectators. (By the way, that's Dan in the middle, in the mud!)

more than 50,000 took part in more than 300 races in the United States (Regenold, 2007). The sport continues to gain momentum.

SO WHAT IS AN ADVENTURE RACE?

Participants of adventure races work together as a unit to complete a designed course and reach the finish line together as quickly as possible. A team is only as fast as its slowest member, meaning the team must work around each teammate's weaknesses. Winners and losers are separated by the psychological demands of meshing as a team (Fisher and Levine, 1999). Strong teams do whatever it takes to help each other, realizing that sooner or later everyone needs help. Less successful teams scoff at weakness, refuse to recognize it within themselves, and "eventually fracture, bicker, and quit" (Burnett, 2001, p. 81).

Only through cooperation and problem solving can the special tests in adventure races be passed. If teams can't complete the special tests, they can't continue the race. It's often beneficial to have both males and females on an adventure racing team. Coed teams tend to finish better than all-male teams because teamwork and stamina are more important than brute strength (Sieger, 2003). Teamwork is so crucial to adventure racing that teams sometimes help each other through a course. Members from elite teams who have already finished will often return to the course to help struggling competitors through tough obstacles (Murphy and McEntegart, 2001). This is a sport that breeds camaraderie even among competitors.

The collective talents and perspectives of team members are necessary for successful completion of each component of the race.

Photo courtesy of Joel Olson

Adventure racing is enjoyed by weekend warriors, family teams of parents who race with their children, police officers, and married couples. Mila and Jeremy Olson of Team Lucky are a husband and wife who enjoy spending quality time with one another while training for adventure races. Mila, a triathlete, and Jeremy, a long-distance runner, are able to share their strengths as they compete as a team during the races. They're constantly looking for their next adventure racing challenge. Almost anyone who is up to the training can find a team and participate in an adventure race. It is a sport for those who want to get out and move. Many teams do races just to see if they can finish, not caring where they place in the standings.

Photo courtesy of Katy Kelley

Husband-and-wife team Mila and Jeremy Olson celebrate completing the Collegiate Nationals—a race that includes paddling, biking, and trail running in the Nevada desert.

FROM ADVENTURE RACING TO ADVENTURE RACING CORE

It's not hard to imagine how students could benefit from doing adventure races in physical education classes. They would get a great workout while learning important lessons about teamwork. Unfortunately, completing an Eco-Challenge in a physical education class is more than a little unrealistic—there would be several risks involved, and it would be very expensive. Most schools don't have access to kayaks, bikes, or other equipment used in traditional adventure races. Many schools are also not located near woods, mountains, or other terrain where adventure races typically take place. The biggest block is that a traditional adventure race covers great distances, and when you have 40 to 50 minutes for physical education class you're limited to staying on or near school grounds.

An avid adventure racer himself, Dan wanted a way to use the basic ideas of adventure racing in a format that could work in a physical education curriculum—without much risk or expensive equipment. The program would use the core ideas of adventure racing. Students would have to work cooperatively in teams. Races would use running as the primary discipline, and teams would be challenged to surmount various obstacles. Dan hoped it would be a racing experience that students would enjoy. The races would be much shorter than an expedition-length adventure race such as Primal Quest or the Eco-Challenge, and even shorter than a sprint adventure race, which typically lasts two to four hours. The race would have

A CORE adventure race can be set up almost anywhere. One good place is your school's track.

to be completed in one class period. Thus, the race would be extremely modified and yet maintain the core ideas of the real deal. With this in mind, Dan decided to call the program the adventure racing CORE, which stands for cooperative obstacle racing experience.

Dan designed and piloted the first CORE adventure race with a middle school class. The students loved it. Instructors saw it as a great way for students to practice cooperation while making gains in their fitness levels. At the request of students and colleagues, Dan designed more CORE adventure races, and soon they incorporated skill practice and concepts as well. Dan's ideas and experiences are presented here in this book, giving you an opportunity to learn how the adventure racing CORE program can be a wonderful addition to your high-quality, standards-based physical education curriculum. Throughout the book you'll see us using the terms *adventure racing CORE*, *CORE adventure race*, and just plain *adventure racing*, but we always mean the same thing.

In a CORE adventure race, students form teams of two, three, or four. They stay in their teams while progressing through a course filled with challenges that must be completed in order to finish the race. In these races, bicycles or kayaks are not needed, unless you have access to them and decide to use them in one of your challenges. You can easily devise races that require no equipment at all (see the Poker Run in chapter 9 as an example). To create variety, you can change the obstacles that racers must complete from race to race; you can also change or modify the location. The most logical place for a CORE adventure race is a track, but if your school has no track you can set up a course on fields, on courts, in the gym, or even in school hallways. To add variety and enjoyment, you can use several different point systems to score the races (see chapter 7). The most athletic teams won't necessarily win or even finish the race. Sometimes a little luck is involved. CORE adventure races are versatile and malleable. In chapters 5 through 9 you'll find obstacles, course layouts, point systems, and races to explore and experiment with on your way to making the most of CORE adventure racing for your students.

2
The Basics of
Adventure Racing CORE

CORE adventure races are easy to put together once you get the hang of it. If you look over the sample races in chapter 9, you'll see the races can vary a great deal. But the majority of races have some basic features in common. Most involve some type of track layout, obstacles to be completed, a question station, judges, and rules that need to be followed. These are the basics of adventure racing CORE.

The standard CORE course consists of four laps of running around a track (1 mile, or 1.6 km), but races can be longer or shorter. In a typical race all teams start with a card that is stamped by a judge whenever they finish a lap. On the first lap teams skip all the challenge stations except for the question station. This helps spread racers out so they're not all reaching the same obstacles at the same time. In nearly all CORE races, teams come to a question station at the end of lap 1, look at the question sign, come up with an answer, and give that answer to the judge. The judge then makes sure the entire team is there together and that the answer is correct. If the answer is incorrect, the team must run back to the question sign before making another guess. If the answer is correct, the team's card is stamped, and they move on. After the first lap, teams continue running, completing every obstacle along the way.

After a team completes a challenge, their card is marked by a judge for verification.

Obstacles may consist of sport skill stations, fundamental movement skills, puzzle building, problem-solving activities, written quizzes, or fitness activities. In a standard race, teams that stay together and complete all four laps around the track, including all obstacles on laps 2, 3, and 4, within the time limit, are finishers. For many adventure race participants, students included, finishing is more important than winning.

Many adults choose adventure races because they want to make their workouts more interesting. It works the same way for physical education students. Adventure racing has numerous benefits and can fit into a physical education curriculum in many ways. Races can replace other weekly runs or cardio activities you might use with your classes. During a sport unit, sport skills can easily be incorporated into course stations. Obviously, CORE races are a perfect fit in units on cooperative games. You can also conduct student assessments through adventure races (see chapter 10). No matter how you use it, CORE adventure racing provides an exciting way for students to benefit physically, emotionally, personally, and socially while meeting physical education standards (see chapter 3).

THE RULES OF ADVENTURE RACING CORE

Every sport has rules, and adventure racing CORE is no different. The following rules apply to all races:

1. Teammates must stay together as a team the entire race.

2. Racers may help teammates, as well as other teams, get through obstacles during and after a race.

3. Judges may not help racers. Students not competing in the race (e.g., because of injury) may participate as judges to help officiate the challenge stations during the race.

4. The only station racers do on the first lap of the race is the question station. Teams complete all stations on every lap after the first.

In addition to these, teams follow any rules specific to the race of the day. We'll discuss rules for specific races in chapters to come.

THE SPIRIT OF ADVENTURE RACING CORE

Once your students have reached the point where they are honest, are responsible for themselves and others, and appreciate the spirit and principles of adventure racing CORE, you'll no longer need judges. This might take a while, and in some classes it might never happen. But if students know this is what you're reaching for, and if you emphasize the spirit of the race in every class, you might be surprised at how they react. To promote responsibility, honesty, and the spirit of adventure racing, have students complete the following adventure racing CORE rubric to self-assess at the end of each race.

Professional Adventure Racer!

I honored the spirit of adventure racing CORE today by . . .

- being honest and responsible for myself and my teammates,
- completing all the stations according to the rules,
- encouraging my teammates in all the tasks, and
- staying with my team throughout the race.

During the entire lesson I did my part to make us a true CORE adventure racing team. I was responsible for myself and behaved respectfully and honorably throughout the race. I even encouraged other teams to succeed!

Semiprofessional Adventure Racer

I tried to honor the spirit of adventure racing CORE today, but I wasn't completely successful. With a little more effort I will be at the professional level next time.

Rookie Adventure Racer

I didn't give enough effort toward honoring the spirit of adventure racing CORE today. But because honesty is so important in CORE adventure racing, I have been truthful in my self-evaluation today. I know I have what it takes to move on to the next level.

Today I was a _____ adventure racer.

Write two or three sentences explaining why you rated yourself at this level:

_____
_____
_____
_____
_____
_____
_____
_____
_____
_____

From D. DeJager and C. Himberg, 2008, *Adventure racing activities for fun and fitness* (Champaign, IL: Human Kinetics).

Judges

Until your students no longer need them, judges serve the following purposes:

▶ To ensure teams complete exercises and problems at each station

▶ To ensure teams stay together according to the rules (e.g., link arms or touch shoulders before they can move on)

▶ To provide equipment as needed (e.g., paper and pens) or to hold a dry-erase board at the question station (so students don't try to cheat other teams by erasing questions as they pass)

Most races require about four judges (one for each station, if you run a single class), but you'll probably need more if you combine classes or if you have many stations in your race. You can involve students who are injured, or who can't participate in the physical activities for other reasons, by having them serve as judges. When you have fewer than four students available to serve as judges, you might have students earn the position of judge. Just don't let the same students be judges too often (unless they're injured) or else you'll sacrifice the health benefits they'll gain by running the races.

A student judge remains focused while monitoring a team's efforts in completing a challenge.

When choosing judges, you might also consider students who exhibit behavior problems in your class. These students might rise to the challenge if they're allowed to judge. You know your students best, so you'll know which students to pick. When judging, students practice responsibility because it's their job to make sure the race runs smoothly.

Recipes and Ingredients

In later chapters we introduce ideas for setting up CORE races in your classes. If you want to think of this book as a cookbook, be confident you'll have enough recipes to last you a while. If you're like us, you'll want to use the recipes as guidelines and put your own personal touch on them. That's your choice. You can use the CORE races exactly as described, or you can add ingredients of your own. As long as you're using appropriate practices and encouraging kids to be active, it's all the same to us!

3
Benefits of
Adventure Racing CORE

The potential benefits of trying adventure racing CORE with your students are many. First, using CORE adventure racing as a teaching method allows you to easily target several standards in one lesson. In today's standards-based educational climate, that's a real advantage. With our six national standards, each focusing on a distinct area of student development, it's great to have a tool in your tool belt that can build students' competence in several areas at once. In this chapter we explain how each of the six national standards can be targeted using CORE adventure racing.

TARGETING STANDARDS WITH ADVENTURE RACING CORE

Providing enjoyment is an important way to help students get and stay motivated in physical education. Before we talk about fun, though (which we'll get to at the end of the chapter), let's look first at how adventure racing CORE can help you meet the National Association for Sport and Physical Education (NASPE) standards for physical education. After all, lessons that are *only* fun and games don't lead students much closer to the most important outcome for physical education—a physically educated person. Our national standards, and our common sense, tell us that to reach this goal we must help all our students develop the skills, knowledge, and dispositions they need to be physically active now and for the rest of their lives.

We want to show you how smooth and natural it is to implement the NASPE standards into your adventure racing CORE lessons (if you also need to target your state or district standards, this chapter should give you a good idea of how to do so because those standards are likely to be similar). As we mentioned, the CORE program allows you to focus on several standards in a single lesson. In the sections that follow we describe generally and briefly how this can be done. We discuss the standards in the order of how we believe they are emphasized in adventure racing CORE.

Targeting NASPE Standards 4 and 5

NASPE standards 4 and 5 are stressed naturally in every adventure racing CORE experience. "Working to develop responsible personal and social behavior while having fun and developing physical fitness" is actually an accurate way to summarize the CORE program. Other ingredients for the different racing experiences will vary, but these two focus areas will always be included in CORE lessons.

NASPE standard 4 states that a physically educated person "achieves and maintains a health-enhancing level of physical fitness" (NASPE, 2004, p. 11). This is an important desired outcome of K-12 physical education, but in many teachers' opinions, it is difficult to accomplish while targeting the other standards. To achieve health-enhancing levels of physical fitness, students need to participate regularly in activities that challenge them physically. Running laps, doing push-ups and sit-ups, and stretching aimlessly can be very boring to students and might turn them off to fitness activities in the long run. Probably the greatest strength of adventure racing CORE is that it's never boring. Students are more likely to associate physical activity with something they *want* to do.

The way most adventure racing CORE races are set up, students get the equivalent of at least 1 mile (1.6 km) of running completed. As students learn the ropes and develop a desire to do more, races can easily be expanded. With highly motivated students and classes, you're usually able to design a variety of race lengths, up to as many as 3 miles (4.8 km) in a single lesson.

Another benefit of using adventure racing in your lessons is that your students will *really* enjoy working on fitness and skills. Not that they don't have some fun already, but most teachers we know who are on the ball (and not just rolling it out) are always looking for new ways to reach their students. Here's what some of the students and teachers who have tried adventure racing CORE have to say:

It mixes athleticism and fun.
Harout, seventh-grade PE student

It's fabulous because it incorporates so many of the standards.
Emmy, high school PE teacher

I really like adventure racing because it doesn't seem like working out.
Jose, eighth-grade student

The best thing about adventure racing is that I can address the standards while the students have fun.
Jen, middle school PE teacher

It's fun!
Elijah, ninth-grade student

More fun than running the mile, for sure!
Emilia, ninth-grade student

I saw some kids sweating for the first time.
Jay, middle school PE teacher

As an elementary specialist I only get to meet with students once or twice a week. Adventure racing CORE lets me include fitness and skill development in one activity, so I can cover more in less time.
Seth, elementary PE specialist

Students running the first lap of a CORE adventure race.

It keeps them moving.
Lisa, middle school PE teacher

I use it all of the time, especially at the elementary schools.
Anne, substitute PE teacher

It's an interesting and better version of the mile.
Brandon, seventh-grade CORE racer

It makes running more fun. Definitely better than running the mile, and I give it more effort.
Misha, ninth-grade alternative education student

I hate running, but when we do the adventure races I forget that I'm running, and it's fun even doing push-ups with my team.
Ashley, eighth-grade alternative education student

It camouflages running.
Jay, middle school PE teacher

I love to see the students sweat and smile at the same time.
Mike, future PE teacher

I have never seen our students put more effort into an activity in physical education.
Lori, alternative education teacher

Adventure racing CORE is a form of interval training. Students run in spurts of 1/16 to 1/4 of a mile (.1 to .4 km) at a time, which can of course vary greatly in time spent running depending on student motivation and physical fitness levels. But generally we're talking about one to four minutes of running, interspersed with a variety of obstacles that focus on health-related or skill-related fitness, problem solving, concept learning, and the learning of specific skills for sports and dance. An interesting thing we have found from talking to teachers who have used adventure racing CORE in their classes is that many students complete the CORE basic course (1 mile, or 1.6 km) faster than they would complete the standard mile run! Maybe that's because students enjoy the variation from the traditional lesson setup, or that they give more effort because they're working cooperatively with their peers.

In our experience, we've seen that students are clearly motivated to move faster, and thus exert more energy, when running the mile CORE style (see figure 3.1). Enjoyment is the key. When students are having fun cooperating with peers, they put their hearts into what they're doing, and that makes a huge difference in several areas. In a study of middle school students' physical and emotional progress, it was discovered that students had a higher average heart rate, took more steps, and had more fun running a mile in CORE adventure races than they did running the mile the regular way (DeJager, 2004).

Other than running faster and for longer distances, students running in CORE adventure races amaze their teachers in their sudden willingness to perform

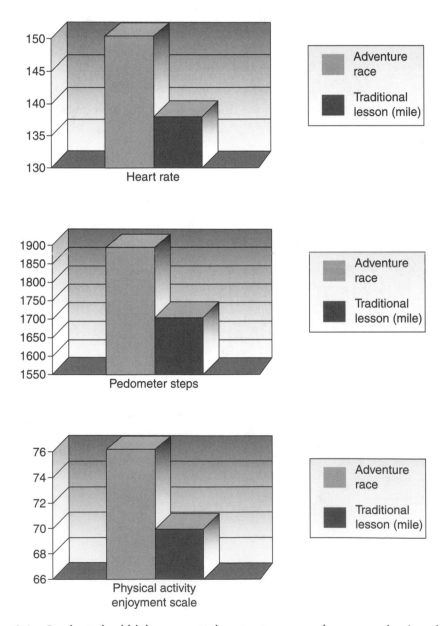

Figure 3.1 Students had higher average heart rates, moved more, and enjoyed adventure racing CORE more than when doing the same exercises (warm-ups, push-ups, sit-ups, running the mile) in a traditional format (DeJager, 2004).

once-dreaded activities such as push-ups, sit-ups, squats, and lunges. Somehow those aren't so awful when placed in a team challenge situation. The transformation of an activity from loathed to loved (or at least tolerated) likely has everything to do with students' perceived purpose and meaningfulness. They're motivated by the teamwork and competition, as well as the interesting setup.

> *I really like how the activities change at each station.*
> Lily, sixth-grade student
>
> *When we do squats and push-ups as a team it's more fun, and I push myself more.*
> Josh, eighth-grade student
>
> *The best part about adventure racing is that we work on our fitness, but it doesn't seem so boring and hard the way it's set up.*
> Katya, eighth-grade student

NASPE standard 4 also includes the learning of concepts related to fitness. You'll find it's easy to incorporate concept learning into adventure racing CORE stations. For example, students might be asked at one station to complete a task sheet to help them figure out their target heart rate for cardiorespiratory workouts, and at a later station they have to explain which types of activities they can do to get their heart rates into their target zone. Or students might read about the FITT (frequency, intensity, time, and type) principle at a concept station and later be asked questions about the principle at the question station. In fact, textbooks such as *Fitness for Life* (Corbin and Lindsey, 2007) are full of fitness concepts that students should be learning in physical education. The CORE format provides an interesting and engaging method of teaching these concepts.

Students take part in a challenge that includes lunges. The focus is on the team's successful completion of the challenge rather than on the monotonous nature of the activity.

Most PE teachers are aware that it's important for them to make fitness activities enjoyable for their students. It's difficult to justify running a boot camp–style physical education class focusing solely on standard 4 when we know that fitness levels don't automatically carry over into adulthood. Activity habits, physical skills, and problem-solving skills and abilities are more likely to influence young people later in life, and will ultimately influence their physical activity levels (Corbin, 2002; Himberg, Hutchinson, and Roussell, 2003; Le Masurier and Corbin, 2006). Knowing how to behave appropriately in physical activity settings is also valuable, as is taking responsibility for behaviors that affect your participation in physical activities. CORE adventure racing promotes the social and healthy living skills that young people will need as adults.

NASPE standard 5 states that a physically educated person "exhibits responsible personal and social behavior that respects self and others in physical activity settings" (NASPE, 2004, p. 11). In adventure racing CORE this standard is the key to success. Students can't be successful in adventure races without teamwork and cooperation, and it takes both personal and social responsibility to be a team player.

If you look at the NASPE standards list of sample performance outcomes for standard 5 for grades 6 through 8 and 9 through 12, almost every single one could be a sample outcome of adventure racing CORE. Adventure racing CORE requires students to make responsible decisions, follow rules, be safe, show self-control, promote leadership, officiate fairly (judges), resolve interpersonal conflicts, and cooperate with diverse members (NASPE, 2004). These important demands all stress NASPE standard 5.

Including *all* students (those with abilities and disabilities) in your lessons is not only a requirement for appropriate practices in physical education (MASSPEC, 1995; MASSPEC, 1998), but is crucial if you want to help students achieve standard 5. Even for well-meaning teachers, inclusion can at times be a challenge. Teachers must always look for activities and teaching styles conducive to including all students as completely as possible in all aspects of the learning experience.

Adventure racing CORE promotes inclusion. In a race, lesser-skilled students might be more appreciated by classmates because they get a chance to contribute to their team in a variety of ways. Dominance in sport skills and fitness levels alone is not (or should not be) enough to win a race. Strengths in areas such as knowledge, problem solving, and cooperation are required for making a CORE team successful, and that means all team members get to contribute and achieve success.

All members of a team share in the satisfaction and feelings of success after completing the station challenges.

To encourage student participation and responsibility, station challenges should be designed to include *all* students. This ensures the ultimate success of the team.

We not only can but should tailor races to the needs of each particular class. For example, if you have a student in a wheelchair in one class, make sure your CORE stations include obstacles and skills that that student can complete, either alone or with the help of team members. Knowledge of adapted physical education comes in handy here; if you need more information in this area, we encourage you to get in touch with an adapted physical education specialist—there should be at least one in your district.

Many physical educators argue that NASPE standard 5 is the most important of the standards because it targets dispositions that are key to being a good human being. There's no doubt that society will benefit from more people being able to resolve interpersonal conflicts, cooperate with a range of diverse members, make responsible decisions, follow rules, be safe, show self-control, and lead effectively. These are all outcomes of standard 5, and adventure racing CORE promotes each one of them.

Targeting NASPE Standards 1, 2, 3, and 6

Although CORE adventure racing most obviously focuses on NASPE standards 4 and 5, the other four national standards can be targeted as well. Which standard you put in focus in a particular race depends on the content of your stations. In the race examples in chapter 9, and in the ideas for race content throughout this book, you'll see how this can vary. For example, in some races you might focus on skill development, whereas in other races the learning of concepts might be the primary focus of your stations.

NASPE standard 1 states that a physically educated person "demonstrates competency in motor skills and movement patterns needed to perform a variety of physical activities" (NASPE, 2004, p. 11). In adventure racing CORE, this standard can be targeted through skill-oriented stations. For example, if you have just completed a unit on ultimate Frisbee in which your students learned four different throws, a station could require them to throw and catch 10 successful forehands with a partner at a set distance before they can move on. This example easily translates to most skills taught in sport and games units. In a way, stations serve as continued practice, or review, but in a fun new format. For basketball, stations could include dribbling obstacles; for volleyball, bumps or sets to a partner; for football, throws and catches. You can even have students revisit a dance move or style they have learned in a dance unit. All you need is the music for the dance. If you taught swing during the dance unit, for example, you could ask students to create a swing routine including five different moves that they must perform for the judge twice. A nice feature about varying the skills you ask your students to complete is not only that they get a good review, but also that different students will remember different skills. This allows the strengths of different students to shine in each race. CORE adventure races can be focused on skill practice or review, but you can also mix in concepts at some, or all, of the stations.

NASPE standard 2, focused on the cognitive domain of learning, states that a physically educated person "demonstrates understanding of movement concepts, principles, strategies, and tactics as they apply to the learning and performance of physical activities" (NASPE, 2004, p. 11). Adventure racing CORE makes for a fun method of teaching concepts (you might agree that traditional lecture formats can get pretty boring). At one station you might introduce your students to a new concept, and then ask questions about it at the question station. If, for example, you want to illustrate a concept about learning, such as "the process of motor learning has three distinct stages: cognitive, associative, and autonomous," you can ask students to read a few short illustrated paragraphs pertaining to these stages at one station. Let them know they'll be asked to explain or answer questions about this concept later on. Then in the next lap, at the questions station, you can ask them to list or explain the stages of learning. In a later race you might have them apply these concepts to their own skill learning by asking them to do a self-evaluation of their own stages for the skills taught in your most recent unit.

To target standard 2 you might also ask students to use prior knowledge to solve problems that you create for them, or to recall information from earlier units. For example, you might have students list from a previous lesson three effective cues for the set in volleyball. Or have them create a new and effective cue to help beginners with their basic golf swing. Or ask questions that review tactics learned in your basketball unit. The stations in the CORE program are great opportunities to review and assess, as well as to teach new concepts. The possibilities are endless.

Arguably the most important standard to target in each physical education class, and the most difficult to achieve in the long run, is the one that summarizes the overall purpose of physical education. Standard 3 states that a physically educated person "participates regularly in physical activity" (NASPE, 2004, p. 11). While a student is enrolled in physical education classes, this standard should be easily targeted if the class meets often enough, the class lasts long enough, and the teacher makes sure there's enough activity time for all students. However, even with effective 40- to 50-minute physical education classes, many students still fall short of the recommended level of daily activity, which is at least 60 minutes (and up to several hours) per day (NASPE, 2004). And a larger problem is that as soon as students complete their physical education requirements, way too many of them become sedentary. So the big question is this: Are you helping instill the desire, skills, and knowledge students need to continue to be active after physical education classes end for good? To address standard 3 you must take physical activity beyond the gym.

Adventure racing CORE can help students become active outside of physical education in several ways. As teachers, we have to be aware of the factors that influence activity levels in young people. Basically, active children are more likely to become active adults (Le Masurier and Corbin, 2006; Taylor, Blair, Cummings, Wun, and Malina, 1999). It makes sense that the more confident and competent mover you become as a child, the more likely you are to experience the joy of being active, perhaps even belonging to a team, and in turn you seek that same joy as an adult. Having confidence in your abilities, knowing how to be active, and being able to set challenging, obtainable, specific goals that have a timeline (COST goals); knowing how to overcome barriers such as lack of time, bad weather, or lack of money and resources; and enjoying the exercises or activities you choose are among the most important determinants for adherence to physical activity (Sallis et al., 1992). The figure on the next two pages summarizes the factors that influence physical activity participation with an easy-to-remember phrase: GET ACTIVE FOR LIFE. If you incorporate your knowledge of these important factors into the design of your CORE races, you'll be targeting standard 3 each time.

In a sense, you can look at the last standard, standard 6, as the one that's achieved as the other five are developed. If students experience positive social interaction and a sense of challenge and fun while involved in physical activity, they are more likely to "value physical activity for health, enjoyment, challenge, self-expression, and/or social interaction" (NASPE, 2004, p. 11). When students develop competence in all the other areas (standards 1-5), their appreciation and awareness of the value of physical activity will most likely grow. Each of the elements of adventure racing CORE described in our discussion of the other standards will help your students reach standard 6. The standard clearly focuses on challenge, social interaction, self-expression, and group membership as a means to achieve this intrinsic value. Adventure racing CORE can provide all these opportunities for students, which makes the experience meaningful and enjoyable.

Our national standards are solid and well researched, and they make a lot of sense. They are not difficult to address if you teach in an environment where students have "opportunity to learn" with instructional periods lasting a "minimum of 225 minutes per week," and with "adequate equipment and facilities" (NASPE, 2004, p. 5). In our opinion, it is every qualified teacher's responsibility to use the NASPE standards in planning and teaching. However, for teachers who work in schools and districts that do not adhere to the NASPE guidelines for high-quality physical education, it can be more difficult to target, let alone achieve, the NASPE standards. When you have 50 to 60 students per class, or when there's not enough equipment or a lack of adequate facilities, CORE adventure racing can help you handle the madness. We're not saying it's okay for schools and districts to create these environments, but rather that reality is sometimes not ideal. Adventure racing CORE is a way to target the NASPE standards even in the most challenging of situations. Remember—the only teacher who ever fails is the one who quits trying!

Goal setting

Help students learn self-management skills, such as goal setting and monitoring, to promote being active throughout their lives.

Enjoyment

Emphasize student enjoyment and interest when selecting activities for your curriculum. Create an enjoyable learning environment by using music and helping all students feel successful.

TV, video games, computer games

Teach students strategies for how to balance recreational time to allow for fun physical activities and limit screen time. Teach them to sneak activity into their TV watching (for example, doing squats during commercials).

Attitudes

Keep the class environment positive. Reward effort. Make PE meaningful by catering to student interests.

Confidence in abilities (self-efficacy)

Plan lessons with variations so that all students can feel successful. Use units of sufficient length so that students can become or feel competent in many activities and proficient in a few. Assess student progress.

Time and other perceived barriers

Teach students to manage their time and minimize perceived barriers in order to fit in physical activity. Teach them to make physical activity fun (e.g., making fitness dates with a friend) so that activity becomes a priority in their busy lives. Teach them to solve problems so they can minimize barriers to physical activity throughout life.

Inclement weather

Teach strategies for being active when the weather forces students inside.

Various perceived benefits

Help students experience the benefits of physical activity that are important to them, such as excitement and having fun, learning and improving skills, improving appearance, and increasing fitness.

Educated about how to be active

Teach students how to be active in their community. Teach self-management and problem-solving skills they need to continue to participate in physical activity.

Reprinted, by permission, from C. Himberg, G. Hutchinson and J. Roussell, 2003, *Teaching secondary physical education: Preparing adolescents to be active for life* (Champaign, IL: Human Kinetics), 15.

Factors and Suggestions for Teachers

Family and peer influences

Involve families in your curriculum. Organize activity days or nights, give physical activity homework that involves the family, and inform family members how to help students become more active. Use peer teaching and modeling, including celebrity peers and information about what they do to stay active and fit.

Older—becoming less active as you age

Teach lifetime activities and strategies for how to be active throughout life. Emphasize realistic options and problem solving for times when life gets in the way (i.e., jobs, children, chores).

Recreational programs lacking

Encourage community activity programs to cater to all youth, not just elite athletes; start a recreational program at your school that caters to all students.

Lack of safe spaces in neighborhood

Teach strategies for being more active in safe places (home, school, church, and so on). Help students and their families organize to create more safe places to be active in the community.

Intrinsic motivation

Cater to students' interests; provide choices. Make PE informational, meaningful, and fun. Emphasize individual task mastery, goal setting, and monitoring. Avoid comparing students to each other.

Facility and equipment access

Work with administrators and the community to keep school facilities open and equipment available at night. Teach students how to be active with limited space and equipment.

Economic status, culture, and gender

Be aware of economic and cultural factors that influence activity; encourage and teach strategies for increasing activity levels for all students regardless of background.

Teach activities that challenge and encompass the interests of both boys and girls. Consider factors such as muscle mass and motor-skill differences in adolescents when selecting units to teach.

Be aware of how society influences activity levels of girls and boys. Make an extra effort to motivate girls, who tend to be less active. Help students develop confidence in their abilities; offer them strategies to become more active by expanding their perceived and real opportunities.

MAKING FITNESS FUN

As promised earlier, we want to discuss the element of fun in your physical education lessons. Targeting national standards with lessons is most important, yes, but that doesn't mean you have to sacrifice what students appreciate most of all—pure enjoyment of what they're doing. Simply put, adventure racing makes fitness more enjoyable for your students.

No doubt one of the greatest challenges physical education teachers face is to make fitness activities enjoyable. The mere thought of running makes some young people cringe and rebel. They often don't realize that people who are regularly active and fit actually *enjoy* what they do in order to stay fit and healthy. And when you try to convince them, they'll likely believe you're trying to trick them into doing something they don't want to do. Another solution is to introduce them to a variety of activities that are fun, and then to show them how these activities lead to fitness development.

> *Doing calisthenics was boring even for me. How could I expect that the students would get any enjoyment out of it? But the same fitness warm-up calisthenics used in the adventure races all of a sudden became fun.*
>
> Amy, middle school PE teacher
>
> *I used to dread telling students to run the mile because of the reaction I would get. Now when I say, "We're doing an adventure race today," I get smiles and mostly positive reactions, even though they run just as far. They definitely enjoy it more.*
>
> Brett, high school PE teacher
>
> *It has been amazing to see a change in students' attitudes toward running and other fitness activities. They actually like it when we do adventure races, even though they run more and work harder on the fitness tasks I give them.*
>
> Jennifer, middle school PE teacher

Students are more likely to put greater effort into activities they perceive as enjoyable. These students are having fun doing high-five push-ups.

Here are some key elements that make adventure racing CORE a fun experience:

▶ Working together as a team to complete a race

Many children don't experience the great feeling of belonging to a sport team outside of physical education. Working together with teammates to complete a race can be a wonderful experience, especially for the many kids who don't participate in youth or school sport programs.

▶ Solving problems together, relying on each team member's unique strengths

Here it's up to teachers to ensure their stations include exercises and challenges that require a variety of talents. This is a great opportunity for teachers to highlight students' uniqueness in the form of their types of intelligence (spatial, interpersonal, naturalist, bodily–kinesthetic, logical–mathematical, linguistic, musical, and intrapersonal). Integrating other subject areas can highlight various types of intelligence, is wonderful for learning, and makes a lot of sense in adventure racing CORE.

▶ Competition

Many kids are motivated to do better when there's a competitive element involved. The cool thing about adventure racing CORE is that the competition fosters teamwork and cooperation. Teams that don't work well together don't do well in CORE races.

▶ Humor

When teachers put extra effort into making one or two of the stations a little silly, students appreciate it. Being goofy is fun. If you don't have it in you, maybe you know a colleague who does. Put that person in charge of a station that brings out a little silliness for the students. For example, this could be a station that has the students do the chicken dance.

Activities like the chicken dance can add some goofy fun to an adventure race.

We could continue to discuss the benefits of CORE adventure races for a few more chapters, but you still might not be convinced until you've tried them yourself. So instead we'll move on in the next chapter to a discussion of how to set up your races. Once you've learned to do that, and then run a few races in your own classes, we're pretty sure you'll be one of the many educators who sing the praises of this exciting and innovative new method of instruction.

4
Setting Up an Adventure Race

One of the most convenient features about adventure racing CORE is that once the course has been set up, the race will run itself, which gives you the freedom to spend your time giving feedback, help, and encouragement. Another nice feature is that you can modify the space, obstacles, questions, or equipment to fit the needs you have at your school. In this section we present the setup for a basic CORE adventure race and explain ways in which the setup can be modified to suit the needs of your program.

THE BASICS: A SAMPLE CORE ADVENTURE RACE

Although you won't need bikes, kayaks, or access to a park, a few elements are essential for setting up a CORE adventure race. You'll need enough space to set up a race and the proper equipment for the obstacle stations you decide to include. You'll also require questions for the question station and judges to make sure racers answer questions and complete obstacles appropriately. The racing teams themselves are the last necessity. Adventure races can also be enhanced through the use of technology and instruction sheets.

Space

You'll need either a track or somewhere else that students can do laps. A standard running track is typically used, but races can also be done in other settings, such as a gym, other areas of the school, or somewhere outside of school. Options for laying out your race are explained in detail in chapter 5. The sample race that we're about to explain uses a track on which students can complete four quarter-mile laps.

Equipment

Once you've decided where you'll hold the race, you need to determine what equipment is necessary for every station in your race. For this sample adventure race you'll need 12 single jump ropes and six medicine balls for every 36 students who are racing. You'll also need mats for the sit-up station.

Other equipment might also be needed for CORE adventure races. What kind of equipment and how much you need are up to you. In most cases, instructors use index cards, a stamp, an ink pad, a whiteboard with markers, and cones to set up the course. In chapter 9 we present several examples of CORE adventure races as well as obstacles you can use in your races. As you look at the "recipes" for races, the equipment ("ingredients") needed for the obstacles and the race is listed at the top. Choose the obstacles and races that work best for you based on the equipment you have access to.

CORE adventure racing challenges can be modified so you can use the equipment you have available.

Questions

Over time you'll want to accumulate a library of questions for your question stations, but in the beginning you'll need a dozen or two so that you don't use the same questions for all your classes. Our sample race has four questions, one for each lap the students race.

Write your questions on a whiteboard and make the first question easy (so that students remain spread out for the obstacles). Make questions more difficult as the race goes on. For more instructions, refer to chapter 8. It's devoted to questions and answers from a variety of disciplines. Until you create questions of your own, use those questions for your races based on the subjects and grade levels you're looking for. Some teachers create questions that correspond to other subjects the students are taking in order to help them prepare for an upcoming test or quiz.

Judges

The next step is selecting judges for your race. For this sample race you'll need five students or other teachers to serve as judges. Choose students who are injured, and also try

challenging "problem" students to be judges during the race. After your students have run a few races and you think they understand the spirit of adventure racing, you might choose to use no judges at all, or only at key stations. More information on choosing judges appears in chapter 2.

One judge each is placed at the push-up, jump rope, and sit-up stations for laps 2, 3, and 4. Judges are there to ensure racers do what they're supposed to do at each station. Another judge is at the question station, where he or she holds up the questions for each lap. It's also that judge's job to make sure that no racers alter the questions or the sign during the race. Another judge is at the answer station. This is the hardest task for judges, so you might consider having two judges positioned there, especially for your first race. The answer judge makes sure the entire team is together (teams need to be holding hands, linking arms, or touching shoulders

To ensure integrity, station challenges are often monitored by student or teacher judges.

at the station). After he or she ensures the team is together, the judge stamps the cards for teams with correct answers to the question. You might also want to add another judge as a timer. This judge would start the timer at the beginning of the race and tell students their times after every lap. Using judges allows teachers to provide feedback and encouragement to students and to help judges or racers as needed.

You might think that using five to seven judges in a class sounds like a lot of students being inactive and not involved in the physical part of the activity. We agree. That is why we recommend using all your injured, sick, or otherwise excused students as judges, and using more only when you have to in order for the race to run smoothly. As explained in chapter 1, once your students have attained the spirit of adventure racing, you might need no judges at all.

Teams

After you have selected judges, the remaining students are put into teams of three, ideally—but teams of two or four will also work. How you do this is up to you. We recommend using coed teams. We also recommend that students don't always race on their friends' teams. Some of the best teams are those on which none of the participants knows each other before the race. You can create teams randomly during class or establish them before the class period, taking gender, personalities, and ability levels into consideration. Once teams are established, give each team an index card for stamping.

> ### Our Experience
> An easy and fair way to divide students into random teams of four is to hand out playing cards. Students match up with those who have the same number or face card that they have.

READY TO GO!

Once the judges know their duties and are prepared to take their stations, the last thing you need to do is ensure that all racers understand the race. You can explain this out loud to all racers at once or, if obstacles are more complicated, distribute detailed instruction sheets to each team. In our sample race, students run four laps around the track; teams must stay together in their groups of three.

For lap 1, teams run a full lap, then stop at the question station to answer a question. Once they figure out the answer, as a team, they go to the answer judge, where they link arms, hold hands, or touch shoulders with teammates (this might sound like a

> ### Our Experience
> Emphasize that team members must stay together during the race. This sounds like a simple enough instruction, but many students aren't used to doing this. If necessary, tell all team members to hold on to one jump rope during the race until they're used to running together as a team.

trivial detail, but it's important to ensure the team actually sticks together) and give their answer to the judge. If their answer is correct, their card is stamped or signed, and they move on with the race. If their answer is incorrect, they must run back to the question sign before coming back to the answer judge to attempt another answer. They can't move on until they give the judge the correct answer. As with all obstacles in an adventure race, teams may

Students link arms and verify with the judge that their answer is correct before progressing to the next challenge.

help one another to complete the challenges. In this case, other racers can help a struggling team with the answers to the questions. (However, it's considered cheating to get answers to the questions from students from earlier class periods.) While running each of the remaining laps, teams stop at the push-up, jump rope, and sit-up stations along the way. During each lap, as a team, they do a total of 20 push-ups, 40 jumps with the jump rope, and 25 sit-ups with the one-pound medicine ball. (If your students are already pretty fit, you can increase these numbers.) Teams are allowed to split up the push-ups, jump-rope jumps, and sit-ups any way they like, as long as they complete the total number of reps required of the team. Teams then continue to the question station to answer a question at the end of each lap. When a team has four stamps on their index card, they cross the finish line. As they finish, team members are told their times and are allowed to get a drink of water, cool down, and stretch while they support and cheer on their classmates. This is also a good time for students to do self-assessment or peer assessment using the rubric provided in chapter 2.

USING TECHNOLOGY FOR ENHANCED LEARNING

Adventure races are meant to be flexible, and part of this means you're able to adapt them to nearly any circumstances, including equipment shortages. However, we also recommend using the equipment you have to its best benefit. If you have heart rate monitors or pedometers, for instance, we suggest putting those to use in your adventure races. Learning can be significantly enhanced by the use of these devices. Heart rate monitors can be used as tools for students and teachers to assess intensity, whereas pedometers are valuable in measuring movement.

Heart Rate Monitors

Giving each racer a heart rate monitor can provide valuable information for the teacher and the student. If your school doesn't have that many heart rate monitors, you might assign one or more per team. Different team members can wear the monitor during different races so that everyone gets a chance to learn how to use one.

Heart rate monitors can be valuable in adventure races. Crowhurst and colleagues (1993) found that monitors provide effective objective measures of exercise intensity in physical education. Monitors indicate how hard racers are working out during a race. Students can see, for instance, that they work out harder during an adventure race than during a mile run. This might encourage them to put more effort into their mile run, knowing they have potential for greater success. Measuring heart rate is also an effective way to assess racer intensity and effort during a race. For instance, a student who walks the entire race might have the same heart rate as that of another student who runs the whole race. Teachers often misjudge intensity and effort; they can measure it more objectively with heart rate monitors.

> ### Our Experience
> Using the high-end heart rate monitors that include fancy modes and functions can distract some students. They spend so much time trying to set their heart rate monitors to the preferred settings that they hardly get to use them. We use only the basic model, which is much cheaper and easier to use, and it gives us all the information we need.

Pedometers

Pedometers measure the number of steps taken over a time period. This number of recorded steps can be used in estimating distance and calories burned during

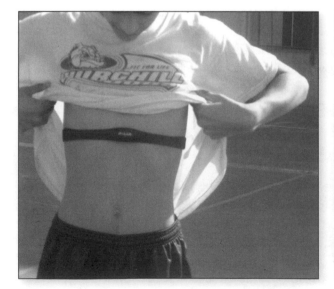

A little technology, such as a heart rate monitor, provides students with a more meaningful learning experience.

Students check their step counts during a race. Pedometers tend to motivate students in an adventure race.

an activity. Pedometers tend to motivate many people to move more because they provide immediate feedback on progress toward goals (Schnirring, 2001).

When all racers wear pedometers, the teacher can assess the amount of movement achieved during a race. This might be used as a way of grading students. Judges can also wear pedometers during a race so that they are encouraged to jog in place or jump up and down while doing their duties, trying to attain the same amount of steps required of the racers.

USING AN INSTRUCTION SHEET

It's often more convenient and efficient to hand students an instruction sheet for the race rather than to try to explain all the details. Instruction sheets allow teams to take a few minutes to look at the race course and the obstacles they'll face, giving them a chance to strategize and determine what they'll do during the race. Providing written instructions also means you don't have to try to talk over students in their excitement for the race that's about to begin. If you use instruction sheets, provide a sheet for every team (not every team member) in the race and tell them they are responsible for consulting it together and returning it when they're finished. Collect the sheets at the end of the race to use for races later in the day. Always ensure that instructions on the sheet are the exact instructions racers should follow during the race.

Instruction sheets should include at least all of the following information: race number (if there is one), race title, race layout, distance of race, special rules for the race (if any), and instructions for each of the obstacle stations. (Sample instruction

Team members receive directions for the race via an instruction sheet. This encourages team building and bonding before and during the race.

sheets can be found in chapter 9.) Each of the recipes for CORE races later in the book come with ready-made instruction sheets to photocopy and give your racers. (Laminate the instruction sheets to make them last longer.) After teams have studied the instruction sheet, you may want to check that they've all understood the key race elements.

TEAM MEMBERS' ROLES

One of the coolest things about adventure racing CORE is that everyone on the team is important. Without everyone on the team working together, a CORE team won't succeed. Every member is important, and every member should contribute toward completing course obstacles. Team members might also be given specific roles, which can be rotated or sustained for several races. Establishing roles for your teams is especially effective when combining adventure races with the sport education model (Siedentop, 1994). For more information on sport education, refer to the book *Sport Education: Quality PE Through Positive Sport Experiences* (1994) by Daryl Siedentop.

Captain

While captains don't choose their teams, they play important roles as team leaders. The primary duty of the captain in adventure racing is to make sure the team is on task, both during the race and during instruction time. The captain also encourages the team to do its best and keeps them going even when they get frustrated. During races, teams might have to make a decision on how they'll run a course or complete an obstacle. In such cases, it can be the captain's job to make these decisions. The captain evaluates and uses all team members' strengths to ensure that everyone is contributing to team success. The most important job of the captain is to do what's necessary to get all team members involved.

Character Coach

Another important role on a racing team is the character coach. Adventure racing is challenging, both physically and mentally. Sometimes teams get frustrated with the race, themselves, or one another. Adventure races give students opportunities to respond to challenging situations positively. The character coach helps promote positive spirit by making sure teammates are encouraging each other. He or she tries to help teammates show appreciation, trust, acceptance, and respect for one another. The character coach encourages high fives, pats on the back, and phrases such as "good job" and "keep going," and they discourage any putdowns.

Equipment Manager

It's the equipment manager's job to pick up and keep track of any equipment the team might need to complete the race; this includes the stamp cards. If heart rate monitors or pedometers are used, the equipment manager should learn their proper operation and share that information with teammates. It's also the equipment manager's job to pick up the team heart rate monitors and pedometers and help set them up with the team on race day.

Statistician

Finally, another team role is the statistician, who is responsible for making sure results are recorded at the end of races at the finish line. This includes telling the teacher (or other recorder) their team number and getting their official finish time. If heart rate monitors and pedometers are used, the statistician should also ensure that the team's measurements get to the teacher for recording or assessment. In addition, statisticians should pay attention to current and past race performances. They keep track of team members' strengths during races so those strengths can be better used in future races. Finally, statisticians encourage their team to improve as the season goes on by paying attention to pacing during races.

Everyone's Involved

You might have noticed that we provided more team member roles than the number of team members we have in our sample race! Using some or all of those roles with your racers is up to you. You might think of roles other than those we've mentioned. Students might hold a role for just one race and rotate with other team members, or they might play the same role for the entire season. No matter what roles you decide to use and how you decide to use them, one of the most important values in adventure racing is that everyone is involved.

Students who are injured or otherwise unable to participate should be appointed judges. If students are in an adventure racing unit and set teams are used throughout the season, teams should take turns judging races. This gives all students the opportunity to experience racing and judging. As mentioned earlier, as students begin to understand the spirit of adventure racing, fewer judges will be needed.

IDEAL OPPORTUNITY FOR TEAM TEACHING

Adventure racing CORE easily lends itself to team teaching. If you have any "roll out the ball" type colleagues, now is the time to get them excited about a new and different activity.

You can work with your department to set up an adventure race for all of your classes during each period, rather than, say, running the regular mile run. You can also work with your department to set up an entire unit of adventure racing. Working with your department is a terrific way to get great ideas for races, and you're less likely to be competing for facilities. Working together also makes race setup much easier. Adventure racing CORE can be done with quite large groups of students—even an entire department can race together.

Our Experience

If you work with colleagues who don't want to be involved in the planning and setup of a race, have them act as judges—and then watch them be intrigued as the race unfolds.

If you choose to team teach, it is ideal for the entire group of teachers to be involved in the planning. One way to do this is to get together

and brainstorm ideas for the race, select the ideas the group likes best, and plan out a race. You can also look through this book and choose a race or get ideas to design your own race. If you're doing a series of races, teachers might take turns planning out races so that everyone gets a chance. If you have a sound system, one teacher might be in charge of compiling music to fit the theme of the race. Music can make a race more entertaining, and sometimes motivating, for both students and teachers.

Designing the race is the fun part. Setting up and cleaning up are not such a pleasure. Split up the tasks. Have half the team teachers in charge of setting up the

equipment for the race and the other half in charge of cleaning up the equipment after the race. You might also get a few student volunteers to help you set up and clean up.

A teacher in the role of starter–finisher gets teams ready for the race.

Our Experience

While it rarely seems to be an issue, it is important to be ready for any traffic jams at a station. You don't want students waiting in line for a turn at the task. To prepare for this, have some extra tasks ready for the groups to do while they wait. Tasks might include extra physical work, such as running in place or doing jumping jacks. Or, you might choose to include a nonphysical race task, such as having teams work on a word find or crossword puzzle.

Students are often happy to help set up because they'll get a sneak preview of the race.

Teachers should each have a job to ensure the race goes smoothly. The teacher who designed the race is usually the best one to explain the race to the students. Another teacher should explain the obstacles to the judges, while another hands out instruction sheets or stamp cards to teams. As teams get ready to head to the starting line, have one teacher be the starter-finisher. This teacher is in charge of starting the race; after that, he or she spends remaining time at the question station (which tends to be the most entertaining station for an observer and also involves the most confusion for racers) until the first team of racers is ready to finish. As the first team comes in, this teacher goes to the finish line and records the results of the teams as they finish, congratulating them on their success in completing the race. Other teachers can either be judges in charge of obstacles or do informal assessments of students on the course.

Afterward, the team of teachers should meet to discuss what worked and what didn't work as well during the race. This should lead to improvement of future races.

5
Race Layouts

One of the elements instructors like best about adventure racing is the variety of course layouts they can use. The most common layout is on a running track, but you don't have to have a track. You can design courses around the blacktop, in the gym, in an area nearby, or even in a remote area that requires a field trip.

AROUND THE TRACK

Having students race around a track is the easiest way to set up a CORE course. Because the area is easy to keep in full view at all times, you can easily supervise all students at once.

As race director, you get to determine how long to make a race. If your track is 400 meters (like most tracks), you might have racers do four laps for a full mile, or just three laps if they're new to adventure racing. Lengthen races by adding more laps, or partial laps. If your school is on a block schedule, with longer class periods, you might have students race a couple of miles for a greater challenge.

If you have a track nearby, use it—it provides ample space, is easy to monitor, and sometimes has preexisting marks that help with activities.

On the first lap of a CORE adventure race using a track, racers don't stop at any of the obstacle stations. This spreads racers out so they're not all reaching the same obstacles at the same time. At the end of the first lap, racers reach the question station and, as a team, give their answer to the station judge. If they're correct, and if the whole team is together, they get their card stamped by the judge and progress with the race. If they're incorrect, they return to the question sign, consider the question again, and come back to the judge with another answer.

After lap 1, students complete all obstacles around the track on every lap until they've completed the amount of laps required. Obstacles may include fitness, skill, or problem-solving challenges (see chapter 6 for examples).

AROUND THE SCHOOL

If you don't have a track near your school, students can run laps around a large field or around the blacktop or playground area. Set up cones to mark the course, and have racers follow the same rules you'd use if they were racing around a track. This layout is ideal for team teaching because it allows for supervision at key positions on the course.

Another way to lay out a course is to have students do one or two laps around the track and then continue the race around different areas of the school (as long as racers don't distract other classes). For a race like this, racers usually have to complete more obstacles, which is good for variety. Remember that on the first lap students don't do any obstacles except the question station, which they do at the end of the first lap. On all subsequent laps students complete all obstacles set up around the course.

A CORE course can be easily adapted to fit your school setting. All you need is enough space to ensure safety.

At the end of lap 2, racers answer a second question at the answer station (make it a tough question). If the answer is correct they move on to the

next section of the race, which can be run anywhere. For instance, you might have students run up from the track, around the blacktop, around the cafeteria, around a large upper field, and back down to the finish line, completing obstacles along the way.

However you set up your course, focus on being safe and creative. Use cones as markers so students don't get confused. A longer course allows racers to complete more obstacles (about six to eight), so it will require more set-up time (again, ideal for team teaching), but the extra time is worth it to watch students work toward their goal of making it to the finish line.

IN THE GYM

Believe it or not, you can use a CORE adventure race as a rainy-day activity inside the gym. You'll need a one-lap course with several elaborate obstacles, or else a multilap course with fairly simple obstacles.

Short Race With Elaborate Obstacles

For an inside-the-gym race with several or elaborate obstacles, place one judge at each obstacle station with a stamp or colored marker (different color for each station). Teams complete the obstacles in any order they wish. Once they have a stamp from every obstacle on the course, they go to the center of the gym to give the instructor their card. Once the instructor confirms all stations have been completed, that team has finished the race. Note that this course follows the "any order" point system as described in chapter 7.

Because the course is so short, the obstacles must be very involved, taking at least 5 minutes each to complete. For example, at one obstacle station, students might be asked to complete fitness or skill challenges. At another station, racers might be challenged to complete a worksheet or a math or science quiz. In this case, the station judge should have a key to the worksheet or quiz and stamp the team's card only when they have all the answers correct.

You can give all students opportunities to shine by integrating subject areas such as English or math into the adventure racing CORE challenges.

Long Race With Simple Obstacles

For a longer, multilap race, students might complete 25 or more laps, depending on the size of the gym and the obstacles used. Fitness stations work well for such a course. Have students weave around cones or jump over short hurdles as they move from obstacle to obstacle. Teams might have to complete 20 push-ups or 40 jumping jacks before moving on. If racers understand and are following the spirit of CORE racing, you can eliminate all judges except for the one marking the cards for each lap that teams complete. If you don't use station judges, it's especially important to mark stations clearly with cones and to display signs explaining precisely what needs to be completed.

In an inside-the-gym race, teams that complete the amount of laps required within the time limit are finishers—and winners. A variation to try with this layout is to give teams a time limit to see how many laps they can complete within a set time. This "as many as you can" point system is explained in chapter 7.

ON A FIELD TRIP

A fun way to lay out a CORE adventure race is to set the race up as part of a field trip. You might design your course at a local park or another safe environment with plenty of space. A field trip is a great way to finish up an adventure racing CORE unit. Students love getting away from school grounds. Just make sure to follow all field trip procedures required by your school.

One of the race directors should get to the site early to set up the course and the festivities. The race course can follow any layout you choose, as long as it's safe.

© Human Kinetics

On a field trip you might provide your students with challenges different from those they can do at school.

Mark the course out with cones so racers aren't confused. Be creative, and have fun. A field trip course can allow for obstacles that might not normally be available. For example, students might walk along the tops of fallen logs or complete a public fitness trail (also called a *parcourse*).

Turn your CORE field trip into a big deal that students can get excited about. Bring out some music. Have a barbecue. Present trophies, certificates, or prizes in a variety of categories (coolest team name, best team spirit, and so on). Give students a taste of what real adventure races and fun runs are like.

Encourage students to take part in adventure races outside of the class experience. Community adventure races with parks and recreation departments are often good sources for outside participation.

There are many ways to lay out an adventure racing course. Use the facilities available to you. Be innovative. This is your chance to break out from the same old same old and plan something of your own design, so take advantage!

6
Obstacles

To carry our cookbook analogy a step further, we consider course obstacles as the spices of adventure racing CORE recipes. The obstacles are probably the main reason students prefer an adventure race to a mile run. Obstacles create the unique flavor of each race depending on how they are combined. It's the obstacles that mix up a race, challenge racers, and give students opportunities to use their talents and knowledge to contribute to their team.

The many obstacles used in races fall into three basic categories: fitness, skill, and problem solving and team building. In chapter 8 we include sample questions to use at the question station obstacles of a CORE race.

In this chapter we explain and present examples of fitness, skill, and problem-solving and team-building obstacles that you can use. You might have seen variations of some of these activities, and others might be new to you. Check them out, and feel free to add your own creative ideas as well.

FITNESS OBSTACLES

The fitness stations in an adventure race give students an opportunity to work on cardiovascular fitness, muscular strength, endurance, and flexibility while progressing through the course. These stations are convenient because you can usually add two or three fitness obstacles to a race with little or no equipment. Plus, once your students understand and buy into the spirit of adventure racing, these stations won't require judges.

Fitness stations typically include exercises that require teams to complete a certain number of repetitions. The team may split the reps up among team members however they like. For example, a push-up station might require 25 reps, in which case one teammate might do 5 and the other two teammates do 10 each. You might be surprised to find that most students will contribute as much as they can to their team.

The following tables each include an exercise, equipment required, an illustrative photo, and the number of repetitions recommended for beginner, intermediate, and advanced teams of three. Some also include variations for the exercise. You may always use your professional knowledge and resources to modify an exercise to accomodate any students with disabilities. Additionally, you may choose to change the number of reps based on your teams' abilities and the number of students on the team.

> ## Our Experience
> Use a number of repetitions that teams can't divide evenly among themselves. This forces the team to solve the problem of how to split up the repetitions.

Bear Crawl

EQUIPMENT	DESCRIPTION	REPETITIONS
Cones	Crawl on hands and feet (not knees). Teams go around cones using the bear crawl.	*Beginner* 5 yards *Intermediate* 10 yards *Advanced* 20 yards

Crab Crawl

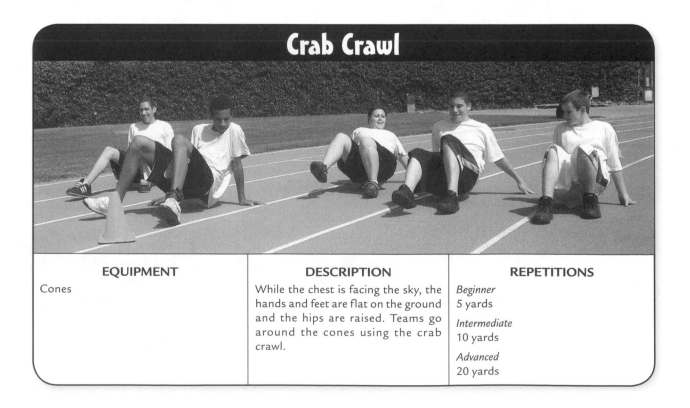

EQUIPMENT	DESCRIPTION	REPETITIONS
Cones	While the chest is facing the sky, the hands and feet are flat on the ground and the hips are raised. Teams go around the cones using the crab crawl.	*Beginner* 5 yards *Intermediate* 10 yards *Advanced* 20 yards

Crunches

EQUIPMENT	DESCRIPTION	REPETITIONS
Exercise mat	Lie flat with knees bent. If hands are placed behind head do not use them to place force on the neck. The main difference between crunches and sit-ups is that in crunches the lower back should not leave the ground.	*Beginner* 35
		Intermediate 65
	VARIATIONS	*Advanced* 105
	Feet in air; feet on ground; crunches on ball; full sit-ups; reverse crunches	

Dips

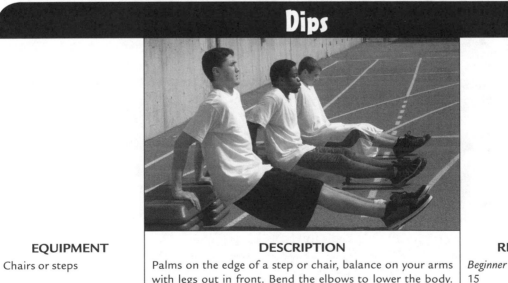

EQUIPMENT	DESCRIPTION	REPETITIONS
Chairs or steps	Palms on the edge of a step or chair, balance on your arms with legs out in front. Bend the elbows to lower the body. Then push back up to starting position.	*Beginner* 15
		Intermediate 30
	VARIATIONS	*Advanced* 50
	Lower steps (makes it easier); legs bent (also makes it easier)	

Flutter Kicks

EQUIPMENT

Exercise mat

DESCRIPTION

Lie on your back, hands at the sides, legs straight. Alternate lifting legs to a 45-degree angle and down again. Place hands under lower back for back support, if needed.

REPETITIONS

Beginner
25

Intermediate
50

Advanced
100

Cross Countries

EQUIPMENT

None

DESCRIPTION

Place the left leg forward and right leg back, as well as the right arm forward and left arm back. Jump in the air, while bringing the right leg and left arm forward and left leg and right arm back. Continue for number of repetitions.

VARIATIONS

Feet closer together (makes it easier); regular jumping jacks

REPETITIONS

Beginner
30

Intermediate
70

Advanced
110

Horizontal Arm Rotations

EQUIPMENT
None

DESCRIPTION
Arms straight out to side. Moving at the shoulder, circle the arms forward or backward.

VARIATION
Use lightweight dumbbells

REPETITIONS
Beginner
40

Intermediate
80

Advanced
160

Jumping Jacks

EQUIPMENT
None

DESCRIPTION
Jump to a position with legs spread wide and arms together overhead. Return to a position with feet together and arms at the side.

VARIATION
Half jumping jacks

REPETITIONS
Beginner
50

Intermediate
80

Advanced
110

Jump Rope

EQUIPMENT	DESCRIPTION	REPETITIONS
Jump ropes	Using your arms turn the jump rope overhead and jump over the rope as it comes down. ## VARIATIONS Use long rope with two turners and one jumper; use more advanced jumps such as alternate foot, crisscross, or double under	*Beginner* 30 *Intermediate* 60 *Advanced* 120

Kick Backs

EQUIPMENT	DESCRIPTION	REPETITIONS
None	Hands flat on ground with both knees touching the ground. Extend one leg back and up (being careful not to over-extend). Bend the up leg and return to the starting position. Switch legs, so they are both exercised evenly.	*Beginner* 25 *Intermediate* 40 *Advanced* 80

Knee Tappers

EQUIPMENT

None

DESCRIPTION

With elbows bent at a 90-degree angle forward and palm facing down, bend one leg, bringing it up to your palm. After lowering the up leg, bring the other leg up.

REPETITIONS

Beginner
50

Intermediate
100

Advanced
150

Lunges

EQUIPMENT

None

DESCRIPTION

With one leg forward bring the front knee to a 90-degree angle (making sure the front knee does not go beyond the toes). Continue until the back knee is nearly touching the ground and return to the starting position.

VARIATIONS

Use steps or BOSU balls

REPETITIONS

Beginner
20

Intermediate
40

Advanced
60

Lunge Walk

EQUIPMENT

Cones

DESCRIPTION

Step forward, landing on the front heel. Bring the front knee to a 90-degree angle (making sure the front knee does not go beyond the toes). Continue until the back knee is nearly touching the ground. Bring the back leg forward into a lunge position. Continue to alternate sides as you move forward. Team must go from one line of cones to the other using lunge walk.

REPETITIONS

Beginner
10 yards

Intermediate
20 yards

Advanced
30 yards

Mountain Climbers

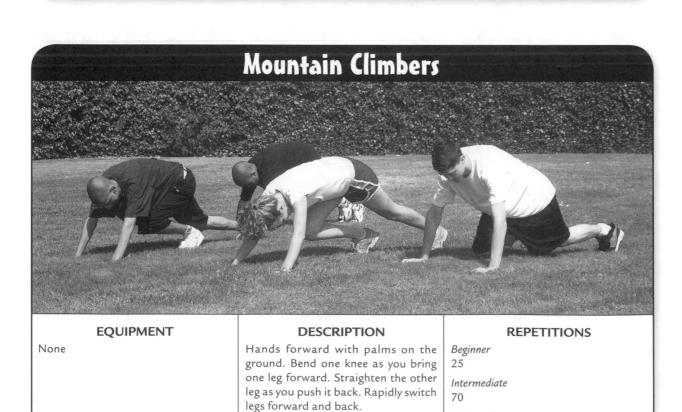

EQUIPMENT

None

DESCRIPTION

Hands forward with palms on the ground. Bend one knee as you bring one leg forward. Straighten the other leg as you push it back. Rapidly switch legs forward and back.

REPETITIONS

Beginner
25

Intermediate
70

Advanced
110

Outside Leg Lifts

EQUIPMENT

None

DESCRIPTION

Lie on your side. Straighten the top leg and using the hip muscles raise the leg into the air. Do the exercise with both legs to ensure equal strengthening.

VARIATIONS

Use body bars or elastic bands

REPETITIONS

Beginner
25

Intermediate
50

Advanced
80

Pop-Ups

EQUIPMENT

None

DESCRIPTION

Start by standing with legs slightly wider than shoulder width and hands on waist or stomach. Drop to a push-up position, bringing feet together. Jump back up to the standing position, widening legs and bringing hands back to the waist or stomach.

REPETITIONS

Beginner
15

Intermediate
30

Advanced
50

Push-Ups

EQUIPMENT
None

DESCRIPTION
Lie horizontal, face down and use the arms to raise and lower the body.

VARIATIONS
Wide, narrow, or diamond hand position; on knees; partner high-five push-ups; arms or legs on step or BOSU ball

REPETITIONS
Beginner
20

Intermediate
40

Advanced
60

Sit-Ups

EQUIPMENT
Exercise mat

DESCRIPTION
Lie with back on floor, knees bent, arms across the chest. Elevate the upper and lower back from the ground, bringing the elbows to the knees. This is a larger range of movement than the crunch exercise and uses hip flexor muscles.

VARIATION
Medicine ball crunches (especially good for students with back problems)

REPETITIONS
Beginner
20

Intermediate
50

Advanced
70

Squats

EQUIPMENT

None

DESCRIPTION

Bend the legs at knees and hips, weight on the heels, and lowering the torso. The torso should remain upright. Straighten the legs to return to the starting position.

VARIATIONS

Wide stance; use body bars or hand weights

REPETITIONS

Beginner
20

Intermediate
40

Advanced
60

Star Jumps

EQUIPMENT

None

DESCRIPTION

Start in a crouching position with knees bent, feet together, and arms in. Jump up and out while widening legs and extending arms. Land in the starting position.

REPETITIONS

Beginner
15

Intermediate
30

Advanced
45

Vertical Arm Rotations

EQUIPMENT

None

DESCRIPTION

Arms straight up above head. Moving at the shoulder, circle the arms forward or backward.

VARIATION

Use lightweight dumbbells

REPETITIONS

Beginner
40

Intermediate
80

Advanced
160

Wall Sit

EQUIPMENT

Wall

DESCRIPTION

Move into a sitting position with legs bent, heels under knees, torso straight up and down, and back up against a wall. Hold the position until the goal time is met. Team must add up times to complete total time. Time starts when legs are in position.

REPETITIONS

Beginner
30 seconds

Intermediate
70 seconds

Advanced
120 seconds

SKILL OBSTACLES

Skill obstacles incorporate skill practice for a sport or activity into your adventure races. CORE adventure races that include skill obstacles can be used as cardio days during a sport or dance unit so that students get cardiovascular activity while having the opportunity to review the skills they've been learning. A CORE adventure race is a great way to end a unit because racers are challenged to perform skills that they've spent the last few weeks learning.

You might ask students to demonstrate skills they have learned in previous units, such as a line dance, for a skill obstacle. A judge can observe several groups at once to avoid students waiting for a turn.

The following tables present sample obstacles for skills in several sports and activities. The listings include the name of the obstacle, equipment needed, and how to set up the obstacle. In general, to avoid students waiting in lines, you should have enough equipment for at least four teams at each station; however, less equipment might be needed for stations that require less time. There are, of course, many more skill obstacles that you can use, but these will give you an idea for creating your own based on the sports and activity units you teach. Choose ours as they are, modify them, or come up with some of your own.

Disc Throw

EQUIPMENT	DESCRIPTION	VARIATIONS
5 or 6 plastic discs, 12 cones (6 for racers to stand behind and 6 to knock over)	Racers stand behind a line of cones and knock over a cone that's 5 to 20 yards in front of them by throwing a plastic disc. If they miss, 1 racer runs out and retrieves the disc. If the cone gets knocked over, it is placed back up, and the disc is brought back to the throwing line before the team moves on. All racers throw at the same time.	Place the cone closer to the throwing line to make it easier and farther away to make it more difficult.

Football Throwing

EQUIPMENT	DESCRIPTION	VARIATIONS
4 footballs, 4 hoops	Racers throw footballs through hoops hanging on a backstop or fence while standing behind a line. Judges toss the footballs back to racers. All racers throw at the same time.	For greater ease, keep the line closer to the hoop; for greater difficulty, keep the line farther from the hoop.

Soccer Passing

EQUIPMENT	DESCRIPTION	VARIATIONS
4 soccer balls, 12 cones	Set up 4 sets of 3 cones in triangle formations 5 to 15 yards from each other. Each team mmenber stands behind a different cone, and the team passes a soccer ball around the triangle. When the ball makes it around the cones 10 times, the team leaves the ball at the cones and moves on.	Bring the cones closer to each other to make passing easier. Require the students to use a certain type of passing to make passes more skill specific.

Line Dancing

EQUIPMENT	DESCRIPTION	VARIATIONS
Portable stereo, CD with selected line dance song	Teams complete 5 full rotations of a line dance to the beat of the music.	Use any line dance that you've taught in earlier units. Have students do more rotations. Ask students to be completely synchronized (you'll need a judge).

Social and Ballroom Dancing

EQUIPMENT	DESCRIPTION	VARIATIONS
Portable stereo, CD with selected social and ballroom dance songs	Teams perform 3 moves they've learned in the dance unit. (Social and ballroom dances include swing, cha-cha, salsa, merengue, foxtrot, tango, rumba, waltz, and more.)	Have students show more than 3 moves. Have them create a new move. All team members must do all moves correctly before they move on.

Golf Pitching

EQUIPMENT	DESCRIPTION	VARIATIONS
8 hoops, 8 golf clubs (pitching wedges or 8-irons), 24 golf balls	Racers chip or pitch a golf ball, aiming for a hoop lying in the grass. When the team has a total of 5 balls in any hoop, they can move on. All racers pitch at the same time.	Bring hoops closer to make the pitches easier; place them farther away to make pitches harder. Increase the number of balls in hoops required to move on.

Tennis Racket Control

EQUIPMENT	DESCRIPTION	VARIATIONS
8 tennis rackets, 8 tennis balls	Students hold their rackets with a proper grip and try to bounce the ball 40 consecutive times. When 1 racer has reached 40, the team moves on.	Ask students to alternate sides of the racket when hitting the ball. Increase or decrease the number of bounces needed. Make a minimum per team member.

Volleyball Bumping

EQUIPMENT	DESCRIPTION	VARIATIONS
2 to 4 volleyballs, 6 to 8 cones	Set up 3 or 4 cones in a triangle or square formation 3 to 5 yards from each other. Each team member stands behind a different cone, and the team bumps a volleyball around the triangle or square. When the ball makes it around 3 times without hitting the ground, the team leaves the ball at the cones and moves on.	Use beach balls to make this easier. Increase or decrease the number of completed rounds of bumps. Have students use 2 balls at once for an extra challenge.

Basketball Dribbling and Passing

EQUIPMENT	DESCRIPTION	VARIATIONS
6 to 8 basketballs, 16 cones	Racers dribble a ball in a zigzag pattern down a line of cones once. Have 3 lines of cones and enough balls for each team member so that there's minimal waiting for other teams who are ready. At the end of the cone line, chest-pass the ball back to the beginning of the cone line to the next team waiting.	Use fewer cones to make this easier and shorter. Use more cones to make this longer and harder.

PROBLEM-SOLVING AND TEAM-BUILDING OBSTACLES

Problem-solving obstacles force teams to use teamwork to find a solution to their problem. These can be challenging, and a lot of fun. Many of these obstacles also include opportunities for teammates to trust one another to be successful. This is where teams that cooperate and communicate effectively will succeed, perhaps

Problem-solving and team-building obstacles are challenging, but they provide opportunities for teams to create successful strategies.

overtaking teams that don't get along as well. Problem-solving obstacles can take a lot of time for teams to complete, or they can be completed quickly, depending on the challenge and the racers.

The following tables show examples of problem-solving and team-building obstacles that you can add to your races. You might have seen some of these activities before, some might be similar to ones you've seen, and others might be new to you. Of course, you can use your own favorite problem-solving and team-building activities as well.

Obstacle stations are what make an adventure race an adventure. These stations allow all students to get involved in solving problems, answering questions, and using their sport and fitness skills to be successful. Many examples of obstacles have been provided in this chapter, but there are many others. Use your imagination and whatever equipment you have to design the obstacles you want in order to achieve your program goals.

Blind Man's Bridge

EQUIPMENT	DESCRIPTION	VARIATIONS
12 cones, 6 blindfolds, 25 to 60 carpet squares, rubber bases, jump ropes, or poly spots (for a class of 48 students; numbers will vary with number of racers and how many obstacles you want them to complete) *Teacher's tip.* If students are uncomfortable about wearing blindfolds, they can close their eyes and look down or cover their eyes with their hands.	Place half the cones in a line across the start of the obstacle and the other cones in a line at the finish of the obstacle. Everything between the 2 lines of cones is the bridge. Bridge length can vary depending on the students and how long you want the obstacle to take (a good starting width is 15 to 20 yards). At the starting line of cones place a blindfold by each cone. Fill the area between the cones with obstacles (the carpet squares, bases, jump ropes, or poly spots). As racers run in to the obstacle, their job is to start at a cone with the blindfold. They choose 1 teammate to be blindfolded and walk with hands out in front across the bridge, from one line of cones to the other. Along the way, teammates may physically guide their "blind" teammate and communicate with him or her so that he or she does not touch any of the obstacles on the bridge. If the "blind" member or any other team member touches any of the obstacles, they must start over.	Several variations can make this activity even more difficult: • Add more obstacles to the middle. • Have all but 1 of the team members be blindfolded. • Teammates may guide only through talking with no touching. • Teammates may guide only through touching with no talking.

Instruction Board

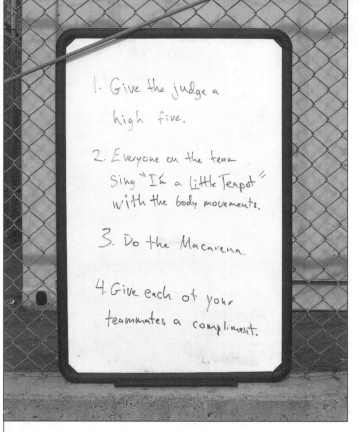

1. Give the judge a high five.

2. Everyone on the team sing "I'm a Little Teapot" with the body movements.

3. Do the Macarena.

4. Give each of your teammates a compliment.

EQUIPMENT

Whiteboard and markers

DESCRIPTION

The instruction board obstacle can be used in place of the question station or as another obstacle on the course. Instructions are written on a sign for teams to complete—one for every lap. Once a team has followed the instructions, team members proceed to the judge to get a stamp to progress with the race. Instructions provide the race director a way to have teams perform many different problem-solving and team-building activities during the race. Here are some examples of instructions you might use:

- Pick up 5 pieces of garbage, show them to the judge, and dispose of them properly before moving on.
- Link arms with teammates and skip to the judge while singing "We're Off to See the Wizard."
- Every teammate gives the judge a high five.
- Every teammate must shake hands with every other teammate in front of the judge.
- Everyone must sing "I'm a Little Teapot" while doing the body motions to the song.

Lava River

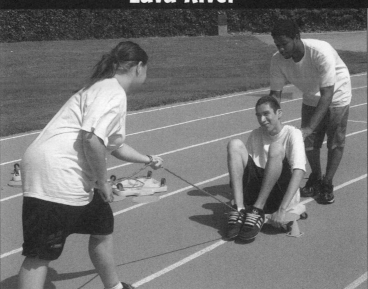

EQUIPMENT

12 cones, 6 scooters, 12 carpet squares or rubber bases, 6 jump ropes (for a class of 48 students; numbers vary with number of racers and type of lava river). Rivers using scooters require hard ground such as blacktop, track, tennis courts, or gym floor.

Teacher's tip: If you have enough equipment for each racing team, have each team carry their equipment during the entire race. This variation calls for a lot of teamwork throughout the race.

DESCRIPTION

Put half the cones in a line at one edge of the lava river, and the other cones in a line at the other edge of the lava river. Everything between the 2 lines of cones is the lava river. River width can vary depending on racers and how long you want the obstacle to take (a good starting width is 15 to 20 yards). At the edge of the lava river, where racers start the obstacle, place a scooter, 2 carpet squares, and a jump rope at each cone.

As racers run in to the obstacle, their job is to start at a cone with the equipment and try to get their team and all the equipment across the space between the 2 lines of cones (the lava river) by using the equipment and not touching the ground. For safety reasons, racers shouldn't be allowed to stand on scooters. If any team member touches the river, the whole team starts over (judges will be watching racers). (Note: Because of the rules of adventure racing CORE, there's a way for teams to combine equipment and work together to get across the river much easier, but teams don't usually figure this out.)

VARIATIONS

Some possible variations to the lava river activity include the following:

- Take away the scooter and add a poly spot instead (adds variety).
- Take away a carpet square and add a poly spot instead (adds difficulty).
- Take away the jump rope and add a rubber fish instead (adds variety).
- Don't allow team members to talk to each other during the obstacle (adds difficulty).
- Blindfold 1 or more team members.

Lily Pad Leap

EQUIPMENT

2 cones, 20 to 30 poly spots

DESCRIPTION

Spread out 20 to 30 lily pads (poly spots) between 2 cones. All team members must get from one cone to the other without touching the ground between. They may step on the poly spots only. If 1 teammate touches the ground, the entire team starts over.

VARIATIONS

Variations to this activity include the following:

- Use rubber bases instead of poly spots (makes it easier).
- Spread poly spots out (makes it more difficult and might promote more teamwork to help teammates across).
- Have racers use a specific movement to get across (jump, hop, skip, or leap).
- Blindfold 1 or more team members (makes it more difficult, requires more teamwork).

Ring of Power

EQUIPMENT

6 rubber rings, batons, rubber fish, or other type of equipment teams can hold onto; 12 large carpet squares or rubber bases; 12 cones

Teacher's tip: If you have enough equipment for each racing team, have teams carry their equipment during the entire race for an extra challenge.

DESCRIPTION

This is another activity in which students will be crossing a "river." Place half the cones in a line at 1 edge of the river, and the other cones parallel at the other edge of the river. Everything between the 2 lines of cones is the river, which cannot be stepped in. River width may vary depending on racers and how long you want the obstacle to take (a good starting width is 10 to 20 yards). At the starting edge of the river, place a ring; place 2 large carpet squares or rubber bases at each cone.

The goal is for teams to start at a cone with the equipment and try to get all members and all the equipment across the river by using the squares or bases and without touching the "water." In contrast to the Lava River, all teammates now must also be holding onto the ring of power (the water ring, fish, or baton). If any team member touches the river, or lets go of the ring of power, the whole team starts over (judges will be watching).

VARIATIONS

Variations for this activity can add ease or difficulty:

- Use smaller carpet squares and rubber bases (more difficult).

- Allow teams to use 3 squares instead of 2 (easier).

- Place equipment in the river for teams to avoid as they cross (more difficult).

- Allow no verbal communication among team members (more difficult).

- Blindfold 1 or more team members (more difficult).

7
Point Systems for Motivation

Adventure racing gives students a chance to experience many types of races. All CORE races involve teamwork and skill, but some involve a little more luck whereas others involve more strategy. As race director you can choose to use different scoring systems rather than the typical race around the track in which the goal is to be the first one across the finish line. Using nonstandard point systems will appeal to some participants. Because these systems often add elements of strategy and luck, racers who don't always do well in traditional racing formats might have increased motivation to race. Many examples of these types of races appear in chapter 9.

ANY ORDER

In an "any order" race, teams complete the same types of obstacles they would normally complete in an adventure race, but they can do them in any order they choose. Stations are set up around a track, field, blacktop, or gym, and students start and finish the race in the center of all the stations. A judge with a stamp is at each station to ensure each team completes the obstacle before their card is stamped. Once they have a stamp from every station, teams go to the race director and show their completed card to finish the race. Obstacles in this type of race should take longer than normal for teams to complete because there's less running than in a normal CORE race. Because equipment is often limited and because it's difficult for a judge to watch many teams at once, use five to eight stations and limit the number of teams that can work at a station at one time. This forces teams to consider the order in which they should complete the stations as part of their team strategy.

AS MANY AS YOU CAN

The "as many as you can" race uses a normal adventure racing CORE format. Obstacles are placed around a course, and racers start at a starting line. Obstacles are the same as in any other CORE race except there's no question station. In this kind of race, racing teams get their card stamped by a judge each time they complete a lap around the racing course. Teams are given a time limit (usually 20 to 50 minutes) to complete as many laps as they can. The team that completes the most laps within the time limit is the overall winner, but all teams that complete the number of laps set for them by the race director are finishers and thus also winners.

POKER

The Poker point system is a fun way to add some luck to a race. This system works much like "as many as you can," but racers get playing cards instead of card stamps. As race direc-tor you'll need about four decks of playing cards for this one (the decks don't need to match). Judges hand one card out to each team as they complete each lap (you can also have a judge halfway around the lap giving a card to each team as they pass; judges should also ensure teams are staying together). Make sure students don't exchange cards with other teams during the race. Judges can also reward teams who cooperate well, encourage others, and race with integrity by giving them extra cards. At the end of the race's time limit (usually between 20 and 45 minutes, depending on time available, student endurance, and so on), students and the race director gather together and determine which team has the best five-card poker hand. That team is declared the winner.

Our Experience

Students love the Poker point system. We've noticed a sharp increase in motivation from some of the students who normally don't get excited about races. They became the "experts" at the end and enjoy the admiration from the other students.

Poker Hand Ranking From Lowest to Highest

Highest card
Pair
Two pair
Three of a kind
Straight
Flush
Full house
Four of a kind
Straight flush
Royal flush

Teams compare poker hands at the conclusion of a race to determine who has the winning hand.

DICE

The Dice system is similar to the "as many as you can" and Poker systems. Here, instead of getting a card stamp or playing card, teams roll a big six-sided die at each of the checkpoints. The number that rolls up on the die is the number of

points that team gets. The judge at the station, who is in charge of watching the die and ensuring teams are together, then writes the faceup die number on the team's racing card (cards might need to be bigger than usual to fit a lot of numbers). To help prevent cheating, judges should use pens that write in an unusual color, such as green. The team's job is to get around the track and roll the die as many times as they can in the time limit (20 to 45 minutes, depending on time available, student endurance, and so on). Similar to the Poker point system, judges can choose to reward teams who cooperate well, encourage others, and race with integrity by giving them extra rolls. At the end of the time limit, teams come together to add up the points on their racing cards. The team with the highest total is the overall winner. This system adds a lot of luck, which helps keep all teams motivated—yes, the teams with the most endurance will have the most opportunities to roll the die, but they might not have the highest score in the end.

The Dice system adds fun to the event and gives teams with fewer physical skills an opportunity to win.

LOCK-UP

The Lock-Up point system makes for a fun race to watch and definitely mixes things up for the racers. This race consists of three or four laps around a track. At the end of each lap, racers report the lap number

and their team number to the judge. The judge then gives them one number to a lock combination. How the teams remember the combinations is up to them. After the final lap of the race, a team will have received all of the numbers to the combination and will run to a backstop or fence, where all the locks are hanging. They find the lock number that matches their team number and then use their combination numbers to try to open the lock. They'll usually need to try several combinations of numbers because judges haven't given them the numbers in the correct order. Teams try to get their lock open and bring it to the finish line within the time limit.

Team members work together to open their lock, figuring out the right combination of numbers gathered at the end of each lap.

For you, the most difficult part of this race is the setup. You'll first need to label all of the locks with the team numbers. Next you'll want to make a table with the numbers of the combinations of the locks for each lap next to the team numbers. The table should look something like table 7.1 (see below).

This table makes it easier for judges to know what to tell each team after every lap (be sure to pick responsible judges for this race, or teams could end up frustrated as they try to open locks with the wrong numbers!). Remember to hang the locks back up on the fence after the race for the next class.

Table 7.1   Release of Numbers for Locks

TEAM NUMBER	LAP 1	LAP 2	LAP 3
1	35	6	25
2	12	29	2
3	4	17	33

Adventure races can have many different formats. If pressed for time or the need to simplify, you can design a typical race in which the first team across the finish line wins. For variety, enjoyment, and greater motivation among participants, you might want to use other systems now and then. We find that the ones described in this chapter work quite well, but don't feel limited—feel free to modify and create point systems of your own.

8
Sample Race Questions

One of the most enjoyable elements of an adventure racing CORE race—for both racers and spectators—is the question station. This is the station where teams get the most held up. If a team doesn't know the answer to a question, they have to figure it out before moving on. This can bring even the fastest teams to a dead halt and allow other teams to catch up. Because of the question station any team can finish first in any race.

Questions can be about anything, but you'll find it beneficial to spend your time wisely and pose at least a few questions for concept learning or review.

Lectures tend to bore a lot of students, and the same concepts you would cover in a lecture, such as health-related fitness, can be inserted into an adventure race as a question (see chapter 3 for details).

Students on each team work together to answer race questions before moving on to the next physical challenge.

Here are some general suggestions to consider when writing questions for question stations.

1. Avoid yes-or-no, true-or-false, or multiple-choice questions. Write questions that have clear answers.

2. Questions should get gradually more difficult as the race progresses. This allows teams a chance to catch up later in the race.

3. Make the first question easy so students remain spread out for the obstacles. An easy first question will allow teams to quickly give correct answers to judges and move on to the other obstacles in the race. If the first question is too difficult, many teams could get held up at the question station, which could lead to overcrowding at future obstacles during the race.

4. Change questions for your afternoon classes so students can't give away answers over lunch.

The worksheets that follow contain examples of questions you may use in your adventure races. Questions are categorized first by subject and then again by grade level. Use these questions if you like, or create your own.

Your questions can be on any subject you choose. You might include questions about math, language arts, science, history, or any other subject. We find that word puzzles are good for encouraging students to use critical thinking. Questions on popular culture might help involve students who aren't normally excited about school. Many such examples are included in this chapter. Keep in mind that some of these sample questions might need to be modified for your students depending on what they have learned in their classes.

Teachers can of course develop their own questions, and we encourage you to do so. Developing questions for races can be rewarding. You get to watch racer after racer be stumped by your question, and then you'll enjoy the unexpected smile of the student who finally comes up with the answer.

Judges provide instructions to racers, clarify rules, and check for understanding before the start of the race.

Our Experience

We find it helpful to talk to colleagues to see what students are learning in other subject areas. We sometimes use race questions to help students study for tests in other classes.

School Spirit

Middle School

1. Take the total number of letters in the last name of your student body president and multiply that number by the number of letters in the last name of the school principal.

2. Take the total number of letters in one of your school colors and multiply it by the number of letters in your other school color.

3. What is the last name of the student body vice president?

4. Take the number of letters in the last names of all the physical education teachers and add them together.

5. Take the number of letters in the last name of your physical education teacher and multiply it by the number of letters in the name of your school mascot.

High School

1. If A = 1, B = 2, C = 3, D = 4, and so on for the letters in the alphabet, find the sum of the numerical values of all of the letters in the name of the school mascot.

2. Take the total number of letters in one of your school colors and multiply it by the number of letters in your other school color; then multiply that number by the number of letters in the school principal's last name.

3. What is the name of the college where your physical education teacher got his (or her) bachelor's degree? (You'll have to have told them at some point.)

4. Take the total number of letters in the last name(s) of the vice principal(s) at the school and divide that number by the number of letters in the last name of the principal.

5. If A = 1, B = 2, C = 3, D = 4, and so on for the letters in the alphabet, find the sum of the numerical values of all of the letters in the last three words of your school's fight song.

From D. DeJager and C. Himberg, 2008, *Adventure racing activities for fun and fitness* (Champaign, IL: Human Kinetics).

Art, Music, and Foreign Language

Middle School

1. Name the three primary colors in painting.

2. Count to six in Spanish.

3. What is the title of our national anthem?

4. What famous painting is known for its smile?

5. Who composed "Stars and Stripes Forever"?

High School

1. How do you say "I am going to the library" in Spanish?

2. Who composed "The Star-Spangled Banner"?

3. What famous artist painted *The Starry Night?*

4. What is the name of the famous chapel where the ceiling has a mural painted by Michelangelo?

5. In painting, what are the secondary colors?

From D. DeJager and C. Himberg, 2008, *Adventure racing activities for fun and fitness* (Champaign, IL: Human Kinetics).

Art, Music, and Foreign Language—Answer Key

Middle School

1. Name the three primary colors in painting.
Answer: Red, blue, yellow

2. Count to six in Spanish.
Answer: Uno, dos, tres, quatro, cinco, seis

3. What is the title of our national anthem?
Answer: "The Star-Spangled Banner"

4. What famous painting is known for its smile?
Answer: The *Mona Lisa*

5. Who composed "Stars and Stripes Forever"?
Answer: John Philip Sousa

High School

1. How do you say "I am going to the library" in Spanish?
Answer: Voy a la biblioteca.

2. Who composed "The Star-Spangled Banner"?
Answer: Francis Scott Key

3. What famous artist painted *The Starry Night*?
Answer: Vincent Van Gogh

4. What is the name of the famous chapel where the ceiling has a mural painted by Michelangelo?
Answer: The Sistine Chapel

5. In painting, what are the secondary colors?
Answer: Green, orange, violet

From D. DeJager and C. Himberg, 2008, *Adventure racing activities for fun and fitness* (Champaign, IL: Human Kinetics).

Word Puzzles

Middle School

1. B
    B O W
        W

2. Dec   ision

3. Eggs
    ————
     easy

4. Teen teen teen teen teen teen

5. e
   m
   e
   n t a r y

High School

1. Oholene

2. Sgeg

3. F   a   r

4. k
   c   ——————————
   i
   p

5. Ablapigsnket

From D. DeJager and C. Himberg, 2008, *Adventure racing activities for fun and fitness* (Champaign, IL: Human Kinetics).

Word Puzzles—Answer Key

Middle School

1.   B
   B O W
     W
Answer: Crossbow

2. Dec   ision
Answer: Split decision

3.   Eggs
   _____
        easy

Answer: Eggs over easy

4. Teen teen teen teen teen teen
Answer: Sixteen

5. e
   m
   e
   n t a r y
Answer: Elementary

High School

1. Oholene
Answer: Hole in one

2. Sgeg
Answer: Scrambled eggs

3. F   a   r
Answer: Far apart

4. k
   c   _____
   i
   p
Answer: Pick-up line

5. Ablapigsnket
Answer: Pigs in a blanket

From D. DeJager and C. Himberg, 2008, *Adventure racing activities for fun and fitness* (Champaign, IL: Human Kinetics).

Popular Culture

Middle School

1. Name the main character from *The Legend of Zelda*.

2. Name Han Solo's sidekick.

3. Name the Teenage Mutant Ninja Turtles.

4. What is Barbie's new boyfriend's name?

5. What is Spiderman's real name?

High School

1. What does the "YM" in *YM* magazine stand for?

2. What is the name of the female Smurf?

3. What game came with the Control Deck bundle of the original eight-bit Nintendo Entertainment System?

4. Who plays the giant in the movie *The Princess Bride*?

5. Who won the Tour de France seven times?

From D. DeJager and C. Himberg, 2008, *Adventure racing activities for fun and fitness* (Champaign, IL: Human Kinetics).

Popular Culture—Answer Key

Middle School

1. Name the main character from *The Legend of Zelda*.
Answer: Link

2. Name Han Solo's sidekick.
Answer: Chewbacca

3. Name the Teenage Mutant Ninja Turtles.
Answer: Leonardo, Michelangelo, Donatello, Raphael

4. What is Barbie's new boyfriend's name?
Answer: Austin

5. What is Spiderman's real name?
Answer: Peter Parker

High School

1. What does the "YM" in *YM* magazine stand for?
Answer: Your Magazine

2. What is the name of the female Smurf?
Answer: Smurfette

3. What game came with the Control Deck bundle of the original eight-bit Nintendo Entertainment System?
Answer: Super Mario Bros.

4. Who plays the giant in the movie *The Princess Bride*?
Answer: Andre the Giant

5. Who won the Tour de France seven times?
Answer: Lance Armstrong

From D. DeJager and C. Himberg, 2008, *Adventure racing activities for fun and fitness* (Champaign, IL: Human Kinetics).

Math

Middle School

1. What is 64,566 divided by 34?

2. If Cami is 3 years older than Toni, and Toni is 5 years younger than Emma, who just turned 12, then how old is Cami?

3. What is the order in which algebraic expressions are to be evaluated?

4. In statistics, what is the most frequently occurring value called?

5. What is the mean of 20, 10, 7, 8, 30, and 15?

High School

1. How many centimeters are in an inch?

2. Draw a sample Venn diagram.

3. A car travels at 60 miles per hour for 30 minutes and at 90 miles per hour for the rest of the 45-mile trip. How long does the trip take?

4. Tashena can paint a house in three days, while Joaquin can do it in six. How long does it take them to paint the house if they work together?

5. How many liters make one gallon?

From D. DeJager and C. Himberg, 2008, *Adventure racing activities for fun and fitness* (Champaign, IL: Human Kinetics).

Math—Answer Key

Middle School

1. What is 64,566 divided by 34?
Answer: 1,899

2. If Cami is 3 years older than Toni, and Toni is 5 years younger than Emma, who just turned 12, then how old is Cami?
Answer: 10

3. What is the order in which algebraic expressions are to be evaluated?
Answer: Parentheses, exponents, multiplication and division, addition and subtraction (Please Excuse My Dear Aunt Sally)

4. In statistics, what is the most frequently occurring value called?
Answer: The mode

5. What is the mean of 20, 10, 7, 8, 30, and 15?
Answer: 15

High School

1. How many centimeters are in an inch?
Answer: 2.54

2. Draw a sample Venn diagram.
Answer: The drawing should show two circles with an overlapping section.

3. A car travels at 60 miles per hour for 30 minutes and at 90 miles per hour for the rest of the 45-mile trip. How long does the trip take?
Answer: 40 minutes

4. Tashena can paint a house in three days, while Joaquin can do it in six. How long does it take them to paint the house if they work together?
Answer: Two days

5. How many liters make one gallon?
Answer: 3.8

From D. DeJager and C. Himberg, 2008, *Adventure racing activities for fun and fitness* (Champaign, IL: Human Kinetics).

History and Geography

Middle School

1. Name the original thirteen colonies.

2. Name the seven continents.

3. Name the three groups of indigenous people the Spanish explorers encountered when they came to America (Central and South) in the 16th century.

4. What area (fraction) of the earth is covered by sea water?

5. Who was the first Roman emperor?

High School

1. What month and year did Germany invade Poland in World War II?

2. Who invented the moveable-type printing press?

3. Which King of England signed the Magna Carta and in what year?

4. What year was the Nineteenth Amendment, which granted women the right to vote, ratified?

5. Where and when did Dr. Martin Luther King, Jr. deliver his "I have a dream" speech?

From D. DeJager and C. Himberg, 2008, *Adventure racing activities for fun and fitness* (Champaign, IL: Human Kinetics).

History and Geography—Answer Key

Middle School

1. Name the original thirteen colonies.
Answer: Massachusetts, New York, New Jersey, Delaware, Maryland, Virginia, North Carolina, South Carolina, Georgia, Pennsylvania, Rhode Island, Connecticut, New Hampshire

2. Name the seven continents.
Answer: North America, South America, Africa, Asia, Antarctica, Australia, Europe

3. Name the three groups of indigenous people the Spanish explorers encountered when they came to America (Central and South) in the 16th century.
Answer: Aztecs, Mayas, Incas

4. What area (fraction) of the earth is covered by sea water?
Answer: Two-thirds

5. Who was the first Roman emperor?
Answer: Augustus (or Augustus Caesar; his original name was Octavian)

High School

1. What month and year did Germany invade Poland in World War II?
Answer: September (1st), 1939

2. Who invented the moveable-type printing press?
Answer: Johannes Gutenberg

3. Which King of England signed the Magna Carta and in what year?
Answer: King John in 1215

4. What year was the Nineteenth Amendment, which granted women the right to vote, ratified?
Answer: 1920

5. Where and when did Dr. Martin Luther King, Jr. deliver his "I have a dream" speech?
Answer: Lincoln Memorial, March on Washington, D.C. (for Jobs and Freedom), August (28), 1963

From D. DeJager and C. Himberg, 2008, *Adventure racing activities for fun and fitness* (Champaign, IL: Human Kinetics).

English Literature, Grammar, and Spelling

Middle School

1. Who is the author of *The Adventures of Tom Sawyer*?

2. Correct the misused homophones: They loved they're new house in there new town.

3. Correct the spelling: Deffinetly

4. Correct all errors: The tree lost it's leafs in autum.

5. Correct all errors: Your emberassing me!

High School

1. How many beats are in an iambic pentameter, and where is it used?

2. Who wrote "Shall I compare thee to a summer's day? / Thou art more lovely and more temperate"?

3. Who wrote *The Color Purple*?

4. Make the possessive noun phrase in this sentence plural: The kid's shoe came off.

5. Correct the grammatical errors: We aim to make our customer's live's easier.

From D. DeJager and C. Himberg, 2008, *Adventure racing activities for fun and fitness* (Champaign, IL: Human Kinetics).

English Literature, Grammar, and Spelling—Answer Key

Middle School

1. Who is the author of *The Adventures of Tom Sawyer*?
Answer: Mark Twain (Samuel Clemens)

2. Correct the misused homophones: They loved they're new house in there new town.
Answer: They loved their new house in their new town.

3. Correct the spelling: Deffinetly
Answer: Definitely

4. Correct all errors: The tree lost it's leafs in autum.
Answer: The tree lost its leaves in autumn.

5. Correct all errors: Your emberassing me!
Answer: You're embarrassing me!

High School

1. How many beats are in an iambic pentameter, and where is it used?
Answer: Five; in poetry

2. Who wrote "Shall I compare thee to a summer's day? / Thou art more lovely and more temperate"?
Answer: William Shakespeare

3. Who wrote *The Color Purple*?
Answer: Alice Walker

4. Make the possessive noun phrase in this sentence plural: The kid's shoe came off.
Answer: The kids' shoes came off.

5. Correct the grammatical errors: We aim to make our customer's live's easier.
Answer: We aim to make our customers' lives easier.

From D. DeJager and C. Himberg, 2008, *Adventure racing activities for fun and fitness* (Champaign, IL: Human Kinetics).

Science and Technology

Middle School

1. What is the colored part of the eye called?

2. What is the name of the fourth planet from the sun?

3. How many calories (kcal) are in one gram of fat, carbohydrate, and protein, respectively?

4. Who invented the telephone?

5. Name the three parts of an atom.

High School

1. Arteries, veins, and capillaries are part of which body system?

2. What is your body's largest organ, weighing about 11 pounds (5 kg)?

3. How many bones are in the human body?

4. How many megabytes make up one gigabyte?

5. What are the names of the three major scales used to measure temperature?

From D. DeJager and C. Himberg, 2008, *Adventure racing activities for fun and fitness* (Champaign, IL: Human Kinetics).

Science and Technology—Answer Key

Middle School

1. What is the colored part of the eye called?
Answer: Iris

2. What is the name of the fourth planet from the sun?
Answer: Mars

3. How many calories (kcal) are in one gram of fat, carbohydrate, and protein, respectively?
Answer: Nine, four, four

4. Who invented the telephone?
Answer: Alexander Graham Bell

5. Name the three parts of an atom.
Answer: Neutron, proton, electron

High School

1. Arteries, veins, and capillaries are part of which body system?
Answer: The cardiovascular system

2. What is your body's largest organ, weighing about 11 pounds (5 kg)?
Answer: Your skin

3. How many bones are in the human body?
Answer: 206

4. How many megabytes make up one gigabyte?
Answer: 1,024

5. What are the names of the three major scales used to measure temperature?
Answer: Celsius, Fahrenheit, and Kelvin

From D. DeJager and C. Himberg, 2008, *Adventure racing activities for fun and fitness* (Champaign, IL: Human Kinetics).

9
Adventure Race Recipes

The possibilities for layouts, obstacles, and point systems you can use for your CORE adventure races are virtually endless. If you're creative, you could probably come up with thousands of combinations. But there might be times when you want to put on a race without having to think of a way to put it all together or to figure out all the equipment you'll need. This chapter is for just such times.

From experience, we know that some obstacles, layouts, and point systems work well together. The following recipes are for themed races that students seem to enjoy. Each recipe lists the equipment, race layout, point system, special rules, obstacle stations, and description of the race. The recipes also come with instruction sheets to photocopy and distribute to racers before the race. (Detailed descriptions of station exercises can be found in chapter 6, and sample race questions can be found in chapter 8.)

Our Experience

To save time and trees, make only one instruction sheet per team, and then collect them at the end of the race to use with your next class.

Before starting, students review an instruction sheet explaining the obstacles, layout, and point system of the race.

Adventure Racing 101

Equipment
6 cones to mark obstacle stations, the start line, and the finish line; 1 jump rope per team; 12 to 24 minihurdles (about 1 foot, or 30 cm, high); 1 whiteboard and whiteboard markers; 1 half of an index card per team; 1 stamp or marker

Race Layout
Around the track

Point System
Teams run four laps around a track, receiving a card stamp at the end of every lap. To complete the race, teams must receive four card stamps and cross the finish line.

Special Rules
For lap 1, teams skip all obstacles except the question station. For all other laps they complete all obstacles.

Obstacle Stations

Station 1: Question station. Teams must answer a question correctly before progressing to laps 2, 3, and 4 and crossing the finish line.

Station 2: 30 push-ups. Each team completes 30 push-ups, which can be split up among teammates however they choose (e.g., 10 push-ups each).

Station 3: 50 jumps with a rope. Each team completes 50 jumps with a rope, which can be split up among teammates however they choose (e.g., 15, 15, 20).

Station 4: One-leg hurdle hop. Team members hop on one leg over hurdles in a line at the side of the track.

Description
This is a great race to start with because it's not too complicated and doesn't need much equipment. Stations are set up in order around the track. Use cones to mark obstacle stations. Hurdles are spread out into one or two lines for teams to hop on one foot over.

Judges are needed for the question station and the answer station, but they are optional for the other stations depending on how well racers follow the spirit of adventure racing. Students skip all obstacles but the question station on the first lap but do all obstacles for every lap afterward. Finishing teams are those teams that complete all obstacles, four laps around the track, and receive all four stamps on their card.

From D. DeJager and C. Himberg, 2008, *Adventure racing activities for fun and fitness* (Champaign, IL: Human Kinetics).

Adventure Racing 101—Student Instruction Sheet

Course
Your team runs four laps around the track and receives a card stamp at the end of every lap. To complete the race, receive four card stamps and cross the finish line.

Special Rules
For lap 1 skip all obstacles except the question station. For all other laps complete all of the obstacles.

Obstacle Stations

Station 1: Question station. Your team must answer a question correctly before progressing to laps 2, 3, and 4 and crossing the finish line.

Station 2: 30 push-ups. Your team must complete 30 push-ups. These can be split up among team members however you choose (e.g., 10 push-ups each).

Station 3: 50 jumps with a rope. Your team must complete 50 jumps with rope at this station. These can be split up among team members however you choose (e.g., 15, 15, 20).

Station 4: One-leg hurdle hop. All team members must hop on one leg over the hurdles that are in a line at the side of the track.

That's your syllabus. Now it's time for Adventure Racing 101.

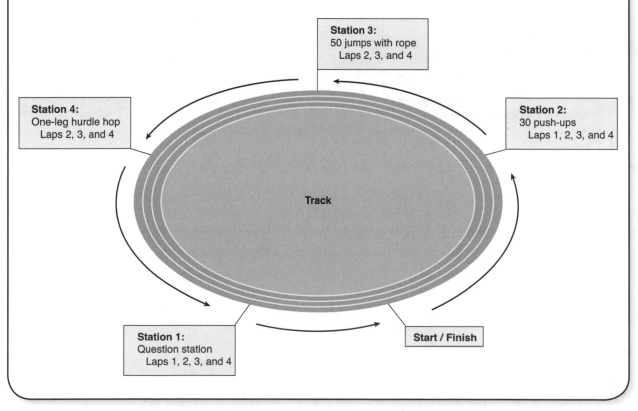

From D. DeJager and C. Himberg, 2008, *Adventure racing activities for fun and fitness* (Champaign, IL: Human Kinetics).

Lock-Up

Equipment
1 combination lock per team (labeled with team numbers); 1 list of combinations for locks; 6 cones to mark obstacle stations, start line, and finish line; 1 whiteboard and whiteboard markers

Race Layout
Around the track to fence or backstop

Point System
Students run three laps around the track. At the end of each lap teams receive a combination number based on their team number. At the end of lap 3 they use the numbers as a combination to open a lock (labeled with their team number) that's attached to a backstop or fence near the track somewhere before the finish line. Teams must open the lock and show the open lock to a judge after crossing the finish line (teams attempting to finish without their lock must go back, open the lock, and bring it back to the finish line).

Special Rules
For lap 1, teams skip all obstacles but the question station. For all other laps, they complete all obstacles.

Obstacle Stations

Station 1: Question station. Teams answer the question correctly before receiving combination numbers after laps 1, 2, and 3.

Station 2: 40 push-ups. Teams complete 40 push-ups, which can be split up among teammates however they choose (e.g., 12, 12, 16).

Station 3: 100 jumping jacks. Teams complete 100 jumping jacks, which can be split up among teammates however they choose (e.g., 40, 40, 20).

Station 4: 40 body squats. Each team completes 40 body squats, which can be split up among teammates however they choose (e.g., 12, 12, 16).

Description
This is a fun race that equalizes the playing field a bit. Students do no obstacles on lap 1. At the end of lap 1 they answer a question and, if correct, are given a number for a combination lock. On laps 2 and 3 racers complete all obstacles and again answer a question to receive a combination number. Using the combination numbers they have received, teams run to a fence or backstop to find where their lock is hanging and then open the lock.

To make the race more difficult, teams can be given their combination numbers in random order. This forces teams to determine the correct order of numbers in the combination for their lock, giving other teams an opportunity to catch up.

This race requires few judges. If teams understand the spirit of adventure racing CORE, there's no need to have judges at the push-up, jumping jack, or body squat stations. Small signs with instructions should be adequate. The judges at the question station must be very responsible because they're in charge of the combinations, and giving a wrong number to a team could leave the team stranded at the lock station forever. This race does take some preparation, including gathering and labeling locks, as well as making a list of combinations that match the labeled locks. The prep time is worth it because this is one of the most exciting races for students.

From D. DeJager and C. Himberg, 2008, *Adventure racing activities for fun and fitness* (Champaign, IL: Human Kinetics).

Lock-Up—Student Instruction Sheet

Course

Your team runs three laps around the track. Following each lap your team will receive a number. At the end of lap 3 you will use the numbers as a combination to open a lock (labeled with your team number) that is attached to a backstop or fence near the track, but before the finish line. Your team must open the lock and show it to a judge after crossing the finish line. (If your team attempts to finish without opening the lock, you will have to go back, open the lock, and bring it to the finish line).

Special Rules

On lap 1, skip all of the obstacles except for the question station. On all other laps, your team will complete all of the obstacles.

Obstacle Stations

Station 1: Question station. Your team must answer the question correctly before receiving the combination number at the end of each lap.

Station 2: 40 push-ups. Your team must complete 40 push-ups. These can be split up among team members however you choose (e.g., 12, 12, 16).

Station 3: 100 jumping jacks. Your team must complete 100 jumping jacks. These can be split up among team members however you choose (e.g., 40, 40, 20).

Station 4: 40 body squats. Your team must complete 40 body squats. These can be split up among team members however you choose (e.g., 12, 12, 16).

Start gathering numbers, it's time to break the code.

From D. DeJager and C. Himberg, 2008, *Adventure racing activities for fun and fitness* (Champaign, IL: Human Kinetics).

Game Over

Equipment

12 cones, 6 scooters, 12 carpet squares or rubber bases, and 6 jump ropes (for a class of 48 students; numbers will vary depending on the number of racers and type of lava river); 20 to 30 poly spots; 6 cones to mark obstacle stations, start line, and finish line; 1 whiteboard and whiteboard markers

Race Layout

Around the track, and then around the blacktop to finish

Point System

Students run two laps around the track and then run up to the blacktop and around the school to complete the course. Students receive no stamps for this race. The goal is to cross the finish line.

Special Rules

There are no card stamps for this race. Teams must complete all stations in order. Teams leaving the course or not correctly completing a challenge are disqualified. Judges determine if challenges are completed incorrectly.

Obstacle Stations

Station 1: Question station. Teams answer a question correctly before progressing to lap 2.

Station 2: 40 push-ups. Each team completes 40 push-ups, which can be split up among teammates however they choose (e.g., 12, 12, 16).

Station 3: 40 star jumps. Each team completes 40 star jumps, which can be split up among teammates however they choose (e.g., 12, 12, 16).

Station 4: 60 lunges (30 on each side). Each team completes 60 lunges, which can be split up among teammates however they choose (e.g., 20, 20, 20).

Station 5: Question station. Teams answer a question correctly before progressing to the blacktop.

Station 6: Lava River. Teams try to get their members and all equipment across the space between the two lines of cones (the lava river) by using the equipment and not touching the ground. Standing on the scooters is not allowed. If any member of a team touches the river, the whole team starts over (judges will be watching). Later teams coming into the obstacle might have to wait for equipment to become available if all stations are full.

Station 7: Lily Pad Leap. Team members must get from one cone to the other without touching the ground in between. They may step on poly spots only. If one teammate touches the ground, the entire team starts over.

Description

The race starts with racers running one lap around the track and answering a question before progressing to a second lap. During the second lap racers do 40 push-ups, 40 star jumps, and 60 lunges. At the end of lap 2, racers answer another question and then progress to complete the rest of the course.

The rest of the course is up to the race director and the facilities available; often it's blacktop area. Once racers reach the blacktop they complete the lava river. After completing the lava river, racers cross the lily pad leap obstacle and head for the finish line.

This race requires a bit of setup because it's spread out and obstacles require some equipment, but the extra effort is worth it because the obstacles promote teamwork.

From D. DeJager and C. Himberg, 2008, *Adventure racing activities for fun and fitness* (Champaign, IL: Human Kinetics).

Game Over—Student Instruction Sheet

Course

Two laps around the track, then around the blacktop to complete the course. Your team will not receive any stamps for this race. The goal is to cross the finish line.

Special Rules

There are no card stamps for this race. Your team must complete all stations in order. If your team leaves the course or doesn't correctly complete a challenge, it will be disqualified. Judges will determine if challenges are completed incorrectly.

Obstacle Stations

Station 1: Question station. Your team must answer a question correctly before progressing to lap 2.

Station 2: 40 push-ups. Your team must complete 40 push-ups. These can be split up among team members however you choose (e.g., 12, 12, 16).

Station 3: 40 star jumps. Your team must completes 40 star jumps. These can be split up among team members however you choose (e.g., 12, 12, 16).

Station 4: 60 lunges (30 on each side). Your team must complete 60 lunges. These can be split up among team members however you choose (e.g., 20, 20, 20).

Station 5: Question station. Your team must answer a question correctly before progressing to the blacktop.

Station 6: Lava River. You must get all of your team members and equipment across the space between the two lines of cones (the lava river) by using the equipment and not touching the ground. Standing on the scooters is not allowed. If any member of the team touches the river, the whole team starts over (judges will be watching). If all Lava River stations are in use by other teams when you arrive at the obstacle, your team may have to wait for the equipment to become available.

Station 7: Lily Pad Leap. All members of your team must get from one cone to the other without touching the ground in between. You may step on poly spots only. If any team member touches the ground, the entire team must start over.

Let the game begin!

From D. DeJager and C. Himberg, 2008, *Adventure racing activities for fun and fitness* (Champaign, IL: Human Kinetics).

Eggstravaganza

Equipment

6 rubber rings, batons, rubber fish, or other type of equipment team members can hold on to; 12 large carpet squares or rubber bases; 12 cones for ring of power; 1 raw egg and 1 plastic zip bag per team; 1 half of an index card per team; 1 stamp or marker for card stamps; 6 cones to mark obstacle stations, start line, and finish line; 1 whiteboard and whiteboard markers

Race Layout

Around the track

Point System

Students race four laps around the track while carrying an egg in a plastic zip bag. Teams receive a card stamp at the end of every lap. To complete the race, a team must receive four card stamps and cross the finish line.

Special Rules

For lap 1 teams skip all obstacles except the question station. For all other laps teams complete all obstacles. The goal is to finish the race while keeping the egg intact and not cracked—teams with cracked eggs are given a 20-minute time penalty.

Obstacle Stations

Station 1: Question station. Each team must answer a question correctly before progressing to laps 2, 3, and 4 and crossing the finish line.

Station 2: 37 push-ups. Each team completes 37 push-ups, which can be split up among teammates however they choose (e.g., 17, 10, 10).

Station 3: Ring of Power. The goal is to start at a cone with the equipment and try to get all team members and all equipment across the space between the two lines of cones (the river) by using the squares or bases and not touching the ground. All teammates must be holding onto the ring of power (it will be obvious what the ring is at the station). If any member of the team touches the river, or is not holding the ring of power, the whole team must start over (judges will be watching). Later teams reaching the obstacle might have to wait for equipment to become available if all stations are full.

Station 4: 150 knee tappers. Each team completes 150 knee tappers, which may be split up among teammates however they choose (e.g., 50, 50, 50).

Description

This race is similar to any other around-the-track race except teams must be "eggstra" responsible and protect their egg during the race. Before the race, each team is given an egg in a plastic zip bag. (Tell them there will be penalties for teams that take their egg out of the bag. The bags help prevent messy spills.)

For lap 1, racers complete only the question station. For laps 2, 3, and 4 they complete all stations. The race requires judges at the question sign and Ring of Power, but not at the fitness stations. The combination of teamwork and fitness elements keeps racers challenged as they try to protect their egg. The race is complete when the racing team has collected four card stamps and crossed the finish line with their uncracked egg.

From D. DeJager and C. Himberg, 2008, *Adventure racing activities for fun and fitness* (Champaign, IL: Human Kinetics).

Eggstravaganza—Student Instruction Sheet

Course
Your team runs four laps around the track receiving a card stamp at the end of every lap. To complete the race, your team must receive four card stamps and cross the finish line.

Special Rules
For lap 1 skip all obstacles except the question station. For all other laps your team must complete all obstacles. Your team races four laps around the track while carrying an egg in a plastic zip bag. The goal is to finish the race while keeping the egg intact without any cracks. If your team cracks the egg, a 20 minute penalty will be added to your time.

Obstacle Stations

Station 1: Question station. Your team must answer a question correctly before progressing to laps 2, 3, and 4 and crossing the finish line.

Station 2: 37 push-ups. Your team must complete 37 push-ups. These can be split up among team members however you choose (e.g., 17, 10, 10).

Station 3: Ring of Power. Your team's goal is to start at a cone with the equipment and try to get all team members and equipment across the space between the two lines of cones (the river) by using the squares or bases and not touching the ground. All team members must be holding onto the ring of power (it will be obvious what the ring is at the station). If any member of the team touches the river, or is not holding the ring of power, the whole team must start over (judges will be watching). If all stations are in use by other teams when you arrive at the obstacle , your team may have to wait for the equipment to become available.

Station 4: 150 knee tappers. Your team must complete 150 knee tappers. These can be split up among team members however you choose (e.g., 50, 50, 50).

Are you ready for this *eggs*traordinary race?

From D. DeJager and C. Himberg, 2008, *Adventure racing activities for fun and fitness* (Champaign, IL: Human Kinetics).

All Sport

Equipment

Football throw—3 or 4 footballs, 2 or 3 hula hoops; Soccer passing—5 soccer balls, 15 cones; Disc throw—5 or 6 plastic discs, 12 cones; Basketball dribbling and passing—3 or 4 basketballs, 8 cones; 1 whiteboard and whiteboard markers

Race Layout

Around the track, and then around the blacktop to finish

Point System

Students race two laps around the track and continue to the blacktop and follow a course to the finish line.

Special Rules

For lap 1 teams skip all stations except the question station. There is no card stamp for this race. Teams complete all stations in order. Teams leaving the course or not correctly completing a challenge are disqualified. Judges determine if challenges are completed incorrectly.

Obstacle Stations

Station 1: Question station. Teams answer a question correctly before progressing to lap 2.

Station 2: Football throw. From behind a line, one team member throws a football through a hula hoop hanging on a backstop or fence. Judges toss the footballs back to the racers.

Station 3: Soccer passing. Each teammate stands behind one of three cones; teammates pass a soccer ball to one another around the triangle. When the ball makes it around the cones 10 times, the team leaves the ball at the cones and moves on.

Station 4: Disc throw. Team members stand behind a line of cones and try to knock over the cone out in front of them by throwing plastic discs. When the cone gets knocked over, it's placed back upright, and the disc is brought back to the throwing line before the team progresses.

Station 5: Question station. Teams answer a question correctly before progressing to the blacktop.

Station 6: Basketball dribbling and passing. Team members dribble a ball zigzag down a line of cones. When done, they chest-pass the balls back to the beginning of the cones to the next team waiting in line.

Description

This race allows racers to practice sports skills they've been learning in other physical education lessons and units. For lap 1, students complete only the question station. For lap 2, they complete the football throw, soccer pass, and disc throw stations. These stations should be set up on the inside or outside of the track where there's plenty of room for the obstacles. Once a team has completed lap 2 and answered the second question, team members move to the blacktop to complete the basketball dribbling and passing obstacle. After completing this obstacle, the team heads for the finish line.

Judges are needed for the question station, but it's up to you whether to use judges for the other stations.

From D. DeJager and C. Himberg, 2008, *Adventure racing activities for fun and fitness* (Champaign, IL: Human Kinetics).

All Sport—Student Instruction Sheet

Course
Two laps around the track, then around the blacktop to complete the course. Your team will not receive any card stamps or punches for this race.

Special Rules
For lap 1 skip all obstacles except the question station. Your team must complete all stations in order. If your team leaves the course or doesn't correctly complete a challenge, it will be disqualified. Judges will determine if challenges are completed incorrectly.

Obstacle Stations

Station 1: Question station. Your team must answer question correctly before progressing to lap 2.

Station 2: Football throw. From behind a line, one team member throws a football through a hula hoop hanging on a backstop or fence. A judge will toss the football back to the thrower.

Station 3: Soccer Passing. Each team member stands behind one of three cones, and you pass a soccer ball around the triangle to one another. When the ball makes it around the cones 10 times, your team will leave the ball at the cones and move on.

Station 4: Disc throw. Your team forms a line and tries to knock over a cone out in front of you by throwing a plastic disc. If the first thrower misses, he or she runs out and retrieves the disc, while the next person in line tries to knock over the cone. If the cone is knocked over, it is placed back upright and the disc is returned to the throwing line before the team progresses to the next station.

Station 5: Question station. Your team must answer the question correctly before progressing to the blacktop.

Station 6: Basketball dribbling and passing. All members of your team dribble a ball zigzag down a line of cones. When done, chest pass the balls back to the beginning of the cones to the next team waiting in line.

Welcome to the sports-o-rama!

From D. DeJager and C. Himberg, 2008, *Adventure racing activities for fun and fitness* (Champaign, IL: Human Kinetics).

Poker Run

Equipment
At least 4 decks of playing cards; 7 cones to mark the obstacles and the start line

Race Layout
Around the track

Point System
This race uses the poker point system. Racers receive one card after completing the first lap of the race and another card for every half lap they complete after that, receiving cards every time they run around the track and complete the push-up and body squat stations. Teams complete as many laps as they can. The more laps and obstacles completed, the more cards the team collects. The more cards the team collects, the better chance of having the best poker hand. The team with the best five-card poker hand at the end wins.

Special Rules
No trading cards with other teams or asking judges for specific cards is allowed.

Obstacle Stations

Station 1: 70 jumping jacks. Each team completes 70 jumping jacks, which can be split up among teammates however they choose (e.g., 20, 20, 30).

Station 2: 70 horizontal arm rotations. Each team completes 70 horizontal arm rotations, which can be split up among teammates however they choose (e.g., 36, 18, 16).

Station 3: 35 push-ups. Each team completes 35 push-ups, which can be split up among teammates however they choose (e.g., 12, 12, 11).

Station 4: 70 mountain climbers. Each team completes 70 mountain climbers, which can be split up among teammates however they choose (e.g., 25, 25, 20).

Station 5: 70 vertical arm rotations. Each team completes 70 vertical arm rotations, which can be split up among teammates however they choose (e.g., 36, 18, 16).

Station 6: 35 body squats. Each team completes 35 body squats, which can be split up among teammates however they choose (e.g., 10, 10, 15).

Description
This race is fun for all students because luck is a big factor. The fittest teams have the opportunity to collect the most cards, but all racers stay motivated to get cards. The race is designed to require minimal equipment. All that's required are a few decks of playing cards, some cones to mark obstacles, and a track of some sort.

If racers have good spirit, this race doesn't require many judges. The only judges necessary are the two handing out the playing cards.

From D. DeJager and C. Himberg, 2008, *Adventure racing activities for fun and fitness* (Champaign, IL: Human Kinetics).

Poker Run—Student Instruction Sheet

Course

Your team completes as many laps as it can. The more laps and obstacles the team completes, the more cards it will collect—and the more cards you collect, the better your team's chance of having the best poker hand.

Special Rules

Your team will receive one card after completing the first lap of the race and another card for every half-lap completed after that (a half-lap card will be given after the push-up and body squat stations). Your team cannot trade cards with other teams or ask the judges for specific cards. The team with the best five-card poker hand at the end wins.

Obstacle Stations

Station 1: 70 jumping jacks. Your team must complete 70 jumping jacks. These can be split up among team members however you choose (e.g., 20, 20, 30).

Station 2: 70 horizontal arm rotations. Your team must complete 70 horizontal arm rotations. These can be split up among team members however you choose (e.g., 36, 18, 16).

Station 3: 35 push-ups. Your team must complete 35 push-ups. These can be split up among team members however you choose (e.g., 12, 12, 11).

Station 4: 70 mountain climbers. Your team must complete 70 mountain climbers. These can be split up among team members however you choose (e.g., 25, 25, 20).

Station 5: 70 vertical arm rotations. Your team must complete 70 vertical arm rotations. These can be split up among team members however you choose (e.g., 36, 18, 16).

Station 6: 35 body squats. Your team must complete 35 body squats. These can be split up among team members however you choose (e.g., 10,10,15).

Time to up the ante!

From D. DeJager and C. Himberg, 2008, *Adventure racing activities for fun and fitness* (Champaign, IL: Human Kinetics).

Cowboy Up

Equipment
1 whiteboard and whiteboard markers; 12 cones; 6 blindfolds; 25 to 60 carpet squares, rubber bases, jump ropes, or poly spots

Race Layout
Around the track, and then around the blacktop to finish

Point System
Teams run two laps around the track, up to the blacktop, and around the school to complete the course. Students receive no stamps for this race. The goal is to cross the finish line.

Special Rules
For lap 1 teams skip all stations except the question station. They must complete all stations in order. Teams leaving the course or not correctly completing a challenge are disqualified. Judges determine if challenges are completed incorrectly.

Obstacle Stations

Station 1: Question station. Teams answer a question correctly before progressing to lap 2.

Station 2: Do-si-do. Each teammate must demonstrate a do-si-do with all other teammates.

Station 3: It's electric! Each team demonstrates a full four-wall rotation of the Electric Slide.

Station 4: Question station. Teams answer a question correctly before progressing to the blacktop.

Station 5: Blind man's bridge. One teammate uses a blindfold to cover his or her eyes while the others guide him or her around a short obstacle course. If the blind man touches an object, the whole team must start over. Once the blind man crosses the course without touching anything, the team continues to station 6.

Station 6: Toss that cow patty. Standing behind cones, all team members toss a poly spot past a line of cones in the field. Team members then continue single file on the sidewalk to the finish line.

Description
It's time to "cowboy up" in this race. Students have an opportunity to demonstrate those line dances they've learned and show off a little square dancing too. They'll have to use some teamwork in blind man's bridge and demonstrate their sports skills when they toss that cow patty. Unless racers are truly in the spirit, you'll need judges for all stations. This is a great race for multiple classes because students can spread out on the long course. The variety of obstacles maintains excitement. This race is a fun one, especially with country music blaring in the background.

From D. DeJager and C. Himberg, 2008, *Adventure racing activities for fun and fitness* (Champaign, IL: Human Kinetics).

Cowboy Up—Student Instruction Sheet

Course
Two laps around the track, then around the blacktop to complete the course. Your team will not receive any card stamps or punches for this race.

Special Rules
For lap 1 skip all obstacles except the question station. Your team must complete all stations in order.

Obstacle Stations

Station 1: Question station. Your team must answer a question correctly before progressing to lap 2.

Station 2: Do-si-do. Each team member must demonstrate a do-si-do with each of the other team members.

Station 3: It's electric! Your team must demonstrate a full four-wall rotation of the Electric Slide.

Station 4: Question station. Your team must answer a question correctly before progressing to the blacktop.

Station 5: Blind man's bridge. One team member uses a blindfold to cover his or her eyes (no peeking!) while the rest guide him or her around a short obstacle course. If the "blind man" touches an object, the team must start over. Once the blind man completes the course without touching anything, the team continues to station 6.

Station 6: Toss that cow patty. Standing behind cones, team members toss a poly spot past a line of cones in the field. After doing so, your team continues single file on the sidewalk to the finish line.

Run to the finish line—*Yee haw!*

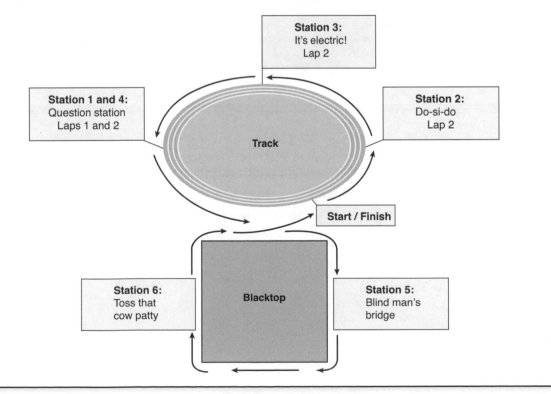

From D. DeJager and C. Himberg, 2008, *Adventure racing activities for fun and fitness* (Champaign, IL: Human Kinetics).

These recipes contain the race layouts, point systems, and obstacles you've seen discussed in other chapters. Using these elements, teachers can develop their own recipes for races if they like, or use one of the races provided in this chapter. Whatever race you choose, feel free to spice up the recipe to meet the needs of your students. The following menu chart might help you choose the right recipes for your class.

	ADVENTURE RACING 101	LOCK-UP	GAME OVER	EGGSTRAVAGANZA	ALL SPORT	POKER RUN	COWBOY UP
LITTLE EQUIPMENT NEEDED	X	X				X	
AROUND THE TRACK	X	X	X	X	X	X	X
AROUND THE BLACKTOP			X		X		X
STANDARD POINT SYSTEM (FIRST TEAM ACROSS THE FINISH LINE)	X		X		X		X
GOOD FOR YOUNGER STUDENTS (K-3)	X				X		
GOOD FOR CLASSES OF STUDENTS WITH VARIED ATHLETIC ABILITIES		X				X	
FEW JUDGES NEEDED	X	X		X		X	

10
Assessment With Adventure Racing CORE

Today's educational climate is not only big on standards (as discussed in chapter 3) but also on *assessment* of those standards. This makes sense because without assessing student learning, how do we know if students are reaching the standards? Assessment, of course, comes down to accountability; teachers of all subjects are constantly being asked to provide evidence that standards are being met.

In this chapter we discuss the importance of assessment, present an overview of different types of assessment, and give you examples of how to assess student learning in all four domains (cognitive, affective, psychomotor, and health-related fitness) through CORE adventure racing. We end the chapter with a reminder that if students use the rubric presented in chapter 2 you're always assessing the affective domain when students race.

ASSESSMENT IS KEY

How do you know whether your students are learning what you intended for them to learn in a lesson or unit? When do you move on to more advanced skills and concepts in your curriculum? How do you know whether students are responsible enough to handle a major challenge? The only way to learn the answers to these questions is to assess your students. If your curriculum is your ship sailing for the port of lifetime physical activity, assessments are the navigational tools to keep you on the right course and help you reach your destination (Himberg, Hutchinson, and Roussell, 2003).

Assessment should be ongoing. You should assess your students at the beginning of a unit to check what they already know and don't know (needs assessment), during a unit so you can give them feedback on their progress (formative assessment), and at the end of a unit to find out the bottom line—What did they learn or accomplish during the unit (summative assessment)? There are traditional types of assessment, such as the Fitnessgram or Presidential fitness tests, written tests, and attitude surveys. These types of assessments are typically separated from instruction and normally used in a summative fashion. Well-designed traditional assessments have their place in a good program—and can be quite helpful—but over the past two decades alternative assessments (also called authentic assessments) have become quite popular with teachers, and for good reasons. Among other important characteristics, alternative assessments focus on the process as much as the product, aim for higher-level thinking and problem-solving skills, and tend to be more enjoyable for students (Herman, Aschbacher, and Winters, 1992). Maybe the most important characteristic of alternative assessment is that it becomes part of the instruction. And that's where adventure racing comes in. It is incredibly easy to infuse alternative assessments into adventure races.

Once your students get used to the basic adventure racing setup, they will want variations. The obstacles can vary quite a bit, as you've seen in earlier chapters, and one variation is to use one or more obstacles to assess student learning from the current or previous units. You can use a race at the middle or end of a unit to check whether students

▶ know the concepts you've taught them (cognitive domain);

▶ can demonstrate the skills they've worked on (psychomotor domain);

▶ progress in exhibiting positive social qualities such as responsibility, cooperation, and teamwork (affective domain); and

▶ have improved their fitness levels (health-related fitness domain).

Some of the ideas we've presented in previous chapters can be considered review or assessment of skills and concepts, depending on whether you collect the results. However, in the next four sections we'll explain the assessment process a little more thoroughly, giving examples for each domain of learning. One important thing to remember is that CORE adventure racing is a group activity, so many of the assessments you conduct during a race will give you an idea of the group's progress, not each individual's. This is especially true for the cognitive domain, where you use questions and problems that the team must solve.

How you choose to use assessments conducted while students are adventure racing is up to you, but we suggest that the best use of this format is for you to assess how well *you* have taught the skills or concepts rather than using this as a formal assessment of student learning that's tied to a grade.

ASSESSING THE COGNITIVE AND AFFECTIVE DOMAINS

It's probably safe to say that in every unit you teach you'll have information that you want the students to learn. This could be the rules of a game, strategy, tactics, concepts of motor learning, exercise physiology, or biomechanics, or it could simply be historical facts of a sport or activity. As students learn the "how to" of motor skills, and know how they feel about their own skill abilities, you might also want to assess their self-efficacy (confidence in their ability), which is part of the affective domain. You can include questions that address any of these areas at the question stations of your adventure races. Here are some examples of concepts that may be taught in a unit, along with corresponding questions to assess the cognitive or affective domains:

Concept Taught

Golf rules state that players must remove the flagstick from the hole when putting on the green, but the stick can stay in the hole (player's choice) when playing shots off the green (e.g., chipping or pitching).

Question

According to the rules of golf, when must you remove the flagstick from the hole? Is it ever okay to leave it in when putting? Explain your answer.

* This is a moderately difficult cognitive domain question that's more effective than true-or-false or multiple-choice questions in finding out if students really understand the rule (because guessing the correct answer becomes difficult).

Concept Taught

Whenever you learn a new motor skill, you go through three stages of learning: the verbal–cognitive stage, the motor stage, and the autonomous stage. (Each stage should be described in detail in class as it is taught.)

Question

What are the three stages of learning? Explain each briefly.

Add-On Task for Individual Assessment

Instructions: On their individual answer cards, team members state what stage of learning they believe they are in for the volleyball set and explain their reasoning. When finished, they hand their answer cards to the judge.

* With this higher-level cognitive domain assessment, you can find out whether each student grasps the concept of learning stages by his or her self-assessment for the skill. In addition, you get an idea of students' confidence in their abilities for this skill, which assesses the affective domain.

Concept Taught

The rhythm for the tango step is slow, slow, quick-quick, slow.

Question

What is the rhythm for the tango step? (cognitive domain)

Add-On Task for Individual Assessment

Instructions: On their individual answer cards, team members rate how they believe they're doing with the tango, on a scale of 1 to 10; 10 is excellent, 5 is okay, and 1 is terrible. When finished, they hand their cards to the judge.

* The first question is a low-level cognitive assessment; it's simply asking students to state something from their memory. The add-on question is an individual affective domain assessment that lets you find out each student's self-efficacy rating for the skill.

Concept Taught

The best position for player-to-player defense in basketball is to place yourself between the player with the ball and the basket.

Question

If you were teaching a fourth grader how to play player-to-player defense in basketball, where would you tell him or her is the best place to position during defensive plays?

* This is a moderately difficult cognitive domain question that's more effective than true-or-false or multiple-choice questions in assessing whether students really understand the tactic.

Concept Taught

The components of fitness are cardiovascular endurance, muscular strength and endurance, flexibility, and body composition.

Question

What are the components of fitness? (cognitive domain)

Add-On Task for Individual Assessment

Instructions: On their individual answer cards, all team members list the fitness component they believe they need to work on the most to reach healthy standards. They hand their cards in to the judge.

* This higher-level cognitive domain assessment tells you if students have the ability to reflect on testing results and come to a correct conclusion with this self-assessment of their fitness level.

Concept Taught

There are safe places in our community where you can be physically active participating in a variety of health-enhancing activities (teacher lists specific places and explains them).

Question

List five safe places in our community that you can be active; name which health-enhancing activities you can do there.

* Although this is a lower-level cognitive assessment question, it can affect students at much higher levels. The answer of course will depend on where you teach. The important thing is that you're assessing students on their knowledge about how and where they can be active in their community outside of school hours, a crucial concept to teach if we aim to increase physical activity levels in youth.

These concepts and questions can be changed according to your needs. Try to be creative in collecting the information you want, while still having a good question for team members to answer in order for the team to advance from the question station.

ASSESSING THE PSYCHOMOTOR DOMAIN

Each time you finish a unit, you might have the same feeling many teachers have—you could really have used more time for assessing whether students learned all the skills you wanted them to learn. After conducting some formative and summative skills assessments, you might have a good idea of student learning, but another chance at checking if the learning really "stuck" is something many of us welcome. Well, an adventure race gives you another chance to find out what your students know how to do, which can help you plan for future units, as well as the next year. If you're using a race to get another look at students' skill levels, the skills station is where you would want to be physically positioned during a race, because you need to see the students' skill performance. You can, of course, video the skills assessment station (using a wide-angle setup on a tripod) if you want to free yourself up to move around more and use the lesson to teach as well as capture video for assessment.

Because the teacher's time is primarily taken up by participating as a judge or facilitator, video provides a record of events that can be reviewed for assessment purposes at a later time.

Here are some examples of skills that you can assess at a CORE adventure race station and suggestions for station instructions. We have provided examples of skills used in individual, dual, and team activities so that it's easier to change them up to suit your needs. Some of these examples are good for assessing cooperation as well (affective domain).

Skill
Soccer dribble

Station Instruction
All team members dribble the soccer ball with their feet, weaving through the cones and free dribbling back for a total of 12 times, with at least 3 times per team member. Each team has one row of cones to themselves. The next team member starts as soon as the one in front is in the middle of the row of cones.

Setup
For minimal wait time, have enough balls and sets of cones set up to accommodate several teams at once. Your space will dictate how many cones to set up for each row, but 6 to 10 is probably enough.

Skill
Line or folk dance

Station Instruction
All team members must perform a dance together for a full minute (specify a line or folk dance you have taught in a previous lesson). The music is continuously repeating, so you can start any time. Once a team has completed a full minute using correct movements and staying with the beat of the music, they progress to the next station.

Setup
All you need is a CD player and enough space to accommodate several teams at once.

Skill
Basketball chest passes

Station Instruction
All team members must pass the basketball to another team member at least 20 times using the chest pass; the total for the team is 80 passes.

Setup
You need enough space and basketballs to accommodate several teams at once. If teams are odd numbered, instruct team members to form a circle for their passing.

Skill
Head stand

Station Instruction
Each team does a total of 90 seconds of head stands, with each team member trying to get the feet up in the air successfully, using correct form as learned in class.

Setup
You need mats and enough space to safely accommodate several teams.

Skill
Tennis serve

Station Instruction
Each team member performs correct technique for 10 mock tennis serves (without a ball).

Setup
You need enough tennis rackets and space to safely accommodate several teams.

A judge is both verifying successful completion of the challenge as well as observing the skill proficiencies of the students at the tennis serve.

Skill
Cardio kickboxing

Station Instruction
Demonstrate correctly and synchronized as a team:

- Eight jabs right and left
- Eight crosses right and left
- Eight hooks right and left
- Four front kicks right and left
- Four side kicks right and left
- Four back kicks right and left

Team members should practice their synchronization because the judge won't let teams progress to the next station until they're perfectly synchronized (the music should help them stay on the same beat). Team members can pass one set of moves at a time (e.g., jabs first, then crosses, then hooks).

Setup
All you need is a CD player and enough space to accommodate several teams at once.

Skill
Swing dance

Station Instruction
All team members perform five swing dance moves while dancing with another team member for 60 seconds. Once the judge confirms that all team members have completed a full minute demonstrating five correct swing moves, staying with the beat of the music, teams may progress to the next station.

Setup
All you need is a CD player and enough space to accommodate several teams at once.

Note that for any partner dance you may modify instructions to give all your students a chance to shine. If you increase the number of moves a team must showcase, for example, you'll probably have a few students who can easily remember 8 to 10 moves, whereas others will struggle to complete 5 correctly. In this case, instructions might read as follows: Teams must showcase 10 different swing moves, and each team member must show at least 5.

Teams demonstrate their swing dance moves in front of a judge.

As you've probably realized, there are many possibilities in choosing skills to assess during an adventure race. By putting skill assessments into this format, you make them fun for students, and students don't feel that they're being tested. More important, assessing during races gives you a chance to have another look at your students to help you decide what skills need to be reviewed more carefully.

Our Experience
Students seem to enjoy and appreciate reviewing what they've learned in previous lessons and classes. When we've done the dance review as an assessment we've been amazed at the cooperative effort they demonstrate to achieve team success.

ASSESSING THE HEALTH-RELATED FITNESS DOMAIN

Traditional fitness assessments such as the Fitnessgram tests are important in any program, but they are often dreaded by students. If you would like to have your students monitor their fitness progress throughout the year without always conducting the tests in a formal setting, you can put the tests into the adventure racing format. For example, if you're using tests from the Fitnessgram battery, you might have students do any of the muscular endurance or strength and flexibility tests at a station. The trick would be in deciding how teams should be rewarded for completing tests to the best of their abilities. After the formal fitness testing earlier in the year, you could have them set goals for improvement, and then in the adventure race you could reward the teams with students who come close to their goals. The reward would depend on the type of race you're conducting. For the poker race, extra cards could be awarded; for the dice race, extra rolls of the dice might be the reward. The main idea is to squeeze the fitness assessments into an enjoyable setting.

Our Experience

Students have expressed appreciation for our efforts to make fitness testing more enjoyable. Many of them apparently notice the effort we've made to switch things up a little—and some even tell us about it.

Students demonstrate Fitnessgram activities within a team context. The concentration is on completing the team task rather than focusing on individual spotlight testing.

You can, of course, use alternative fitness tests in the adventure race. For example, if you have heart rate monitors, you can have students write down their heart rates at the start of each station and reward teams for staying in their target heart rate zone throughout a race.

Students review the data collected by their heart rate monitors, which were worn throughout the race.

CONTINUING ASSESSMENT WITH ADVENTURE RACING CORE

The spirit of adventure racing CORE was described in chapter 2, and a rubric was presented for teachers and students to use in assessing affective domain attributes. If you take a look at that rubric again, you'll see that you can use it to assess learning and growth in the affective domain every time you do an adventure race. Social qualities such as cooperation and teamwork are key components of CORE adventure racing, as well as honesty, responsibility, integrity, and honor. A team that doesn't cooperate in a responsible manner won't succeed. A team that cheats won't have fun. This is what adventure racing is really all about, even though we weave in skills, concepts, and fitness all over the course. If you use debriefing after each race (see chapter 11), you may find that adventure racing can be one of your best methods for assessing NASPE standard 5 as well as any of your state standards that focus on affective learning.

11
Teaching Effectively With Adventure Racing CORE

As you've probably figured out by now, adventure racing CORE is not just another new activity. We think of it more as a teaching style in which you decide the content of the lesson. The possibilities for teaching skills and concepts in this format are endless, and they can be done while students work on much-needed fitness components and social qualities. Best of all, the activities are great fun for the students.

However, as with any lesson, the content does not teach itself. You'll need to use effective teaching strategies for optimal learning and make sure that you always provide a chance for students to reflect on what they have experienced and learned. Some days this can be very brief; students can simply complete the rubric presented in chapter 2. On other days you might need more time to debrief.

REMEMBER YOUR EFFECTIVE TEACHING STRATEGIES

As in any physical education lesson, when you use the CORE format, you aim to be the most effective teacher you can be. This means that you're caring, but demanding, and that you use your time wisely. You provide proper instruction and directions for the stations while keeping it short and simple (the KISS principle), and you always check for understanding of key points. You give cues and feedback when appropriate, minimizing cues to no more than a couple at a time and ensuring feedback is congruent with the cues. You aim to make sure all students are involved in the learning activities at all times. You set up your stations so that all students are challenged but still have chances for

Our Experience

If there are stations for which you know waiting will be required (i.e., there's no way around it, and the learning activity is worth it), we have found it useful to give students a problem at the beginning of the race and ask them to work on the solution at any time they find themselves waiting. The problem might be a word search or crossword puzzle related to concepts you have taught in previous lessons. (Just make sure students don't run with sharp pencils!)

Keeping students active for a majority of the lesson is an important goal in CORE adventure racing.

success. When applicable, you help students set and work toward reaching challenging, obtainable, specific goals that have a timeline (COST) (Himberg, Hutchinson, and Roussell, 2003).

At the end of each lesson, help students understand why they just spent 30 to 50 minutes racing each other, performing all of these obstacles while trying to work together as a team. Help them tie everything together in a brief but meaningful closure.

DEBRIEFING

Children come to your classes with varied experiences and all sorts of baggage. Some have been raised to be honest, polite, cooperative, and supportive of others. Others have never been presented with clear guidelines for right and wrong and might need help developing their moral compass. Usually when you first present activities to your students that are heavy on integrity, honesty, teamwork, and cooperation, it's necessary to address these concepts and attributes in a reflective debriefing after the activity. The CORE program provides many teachable moments, with both positive and negative examples to discuss in order to deepen the understanding and build character in your students.

Teachers unaccustomed to debriefing try to address the "issues" they observed in a race. A common problem is that they hurry through their explanation, thinking they must provide the answers if students can't or won't talk. If you ask students

A teacher takes time following a race to debrief students on the purposes of the activities, inviting comments and insights from the students.

to reflect on an issue or a question, you need to give them time to do so. A useful technique is to have students fill out the CORE rubric (see chapter 2), and then write their thoughts or responses to your questions on the back. Then ask them to share their thoughts with a partner. After this, it's easier to get them to share with the rest of the group.

Most important, you should not provide the answers to your own questions that are aimed at making the students think—at least not right away. Make them think as a homework assignment, and see if you can't get them to share more thoughts the next day. It might take a while to get students who are accustomed to teachers professing to have all the answers to understand that you really do want them to think and share their thoughts with the rest of the group.

Once students are ready (and this might take a while if you encounter problems), you can put a team in charge of the debriefing for the day. This could be the team who finished first, last, or in the middle. It might be a team that you noticed did something noteworthy, either positive or negative. Judges might also take part in debriefing.

Our Experience

We have found that students like to talk about issues related to responsibility, honor, integrity, cooperation, and honesty. Our experience with alternative education students is that they are especially willing to talk and that they have a lot to say! But it takes time to develop the trust necessary for students to understand that you really do care about what they have to say. So don't give up if things don't go well the first few times you try.

Debriefing is important in order to ensure students reflect on and learn from the things that happen while racing. If you want to help students meet NASPE standard 5 (personal and social responsibility), you must help them understand what they're doing that reflects the appropriate development for this standard. Don't assume that they know how to change irresponsible, unsafe, immoral, dishonest, or cruel behaviors. Teach them how during your debriefing by helping them wake up and listen to the wise voices they each have inside. Over time, we hope all your students understand that adventure racing CORE is about so much more than just winning or finishing a race.

12

Beyond PE

Today's physical education teachers are expected to provide students not only with quality, standards-based physical education during school hours, but also to help students get sufficient physical activity outside of school. NASPE standard 3 states that a physically educated person is physically active, and in many professionals' view this is the end goal of the five other standards. Ultimately, this is why we teach students physical education: to help them become physically active now and for the rest of their lives. Of course this brings on extra challenges and responsibilities for physical education teachers and others who work to help children increase activity levels. New ideas are always being sought, and we believe that adventure racing provides many possibilities to help kids become active, and also perhaps to gain a sense of appreciation for physical activity that will stay with them once they have moved beyond our classes.

LOTS OF POSSIBILITIES

We hope in previous chapters we've convinced you that the adventure racing CORE program fits well in any physical education curriculum focusing on the NASPE standards. But you can also use the CORE program in other ways. With adventure racing, you can add a new twist to family fun nights, intramurals, fund-raising, and other special events.

Family Fun Nights

Helping students to become physically active now and for the rest of their lives involves efforts beyond the gym. It has become imperative that physical education teachers connect with students' families. Parents and siblings influence students through modeling, encouraging, supporting, and accommodating physical activity (Sallis et al., 1992). A great way to encourage physical activity for students and their families is through an activity-oriented family fun night. By promoting physical activity for the whole family, you help students reap benefits from the experience far beyond the event. Adventure racing CORE can be the perfect setup. You'll need to modify stations to make sure you accommodate varying ages, from young children to elderly grandparents, but you can have your students help with this once they're familiar with the adventure racing format.

Intramurals

Students need opportunities to be physically active, and not all of them are athletically gifted enough to make the sports team of their choice in school. Even when a team's coach welcomes everyone who's willing to play, without success and playing time many students give up. Intramurals are an opportunity for students who want to be active in an atmosphere of friendly competition. CORE adventure races can be easily incorporated into an intramurals schedule. Students will benefit from the fitness aspects and have fun during friendly competition in which anyone on the team might turn out to be the most valuable member.

Raising Funds

If you find yourself repeating the same boring fund-raising events year after year, and they are only semi-successful, why not try something new? Ask local businesses and organizations to field teams or sponsor teams, or simply to advertise at a CORE event. Using any of the basic races we've introduced in previous chapters, you can create themed races that cater to nearly any audience. If you're raising funds for a team, have athletes help design the race. Participants could pay a flat fee to race, and selling food, drinks, and T-shirts with a cool event-related message would boost revenue.

Special Events

Many schools put on health or wellness fairs, school carnivals, or other special events. Why not promote the great things you do as a physical educator by holding an adventure race? You could make the question station all about your program, including content that you teach, state and national standards, and trivia questions about your students.

Beyond Public Schools

The many ways to use adventure racing CORE extend beyond physical education classes and related events in public schools. All the ideas in this book can easily be modified to fit objectives for events in the college, corporate, religious, or recreational world. The CORE setup can be used in college during freshman orientation, in University Life classes, or in recreational sports programs. Corporations might use adventure racing for team building or training. Religious groups may find the setup enticing for various social events aimed at recruiting young people. Parks and recreation centers could try adventure racing as a new team fitness activity for community members of all ages. All that must be done in any of these cases is to modify race content to match and to appeal to participants. Instead of using physical education standards to guide content, other goals and objectives would come into play. Teamwork, cooperation, responsibility, honor, and integrity are attributes that all individuals could further develop—to their own benefit and to that of their organization.

Adventure races such as the Collegiate Nationals can be an inspiration for University Life type courses, but adventure racing CORE is more likely to suit the needs and abilities of college students.

SHARE YOUR IDEAS AND EXPERIENCES

We hope we have made it clear that the ideas presented in this book are just that—ideas. If you get your creative juices flowing and collaborate with colleagues who are also interested in helping students become active for life, you might find that you'll create enough new ideas for adventure racing to fill a book of your own. In any case, we'd love to hear from you with your thoughts—and success stories!—about adventure racing CORE once you try it. Please contact Dan through either regular mail or e-mail:

Dan DeJager
5236 Lost Creek Road
Shingle Springs, CA 95682
E-mail: adventureracingcore@gmail.com

We'll include the best ideas we receive in the second edition of this book. Also please send along any student feedback you receive. It's always great to hear from young people regarding what's fun, challenging, meaningful, empowering, and exciting for them. We need this information, so let us know!

As you're using this book to enhance your physical education or activity program for young people, we hope you always remember the important role you play in helping your students learn and acquire the skills, knowledge, and dispositions they need to be physically active now and the rest of their lives. You're part of an infrastructure often overlooked when it comes to creating solutions to societal problems such as obesity, bullying, and lack of personal responsibility. One teacher can't do it all, and one activity or program can't either, but a curriculum centered on district, state, and NASPE standards and focused on the goal of helping young people become and stay active can reap benefits in ways that many people don't recognize.

Also, as you do your best every day to make a difference for kids, don't forget to tell key people about what you do. You'll get more support for your efforts if you help administrators, parents, and the public understand that you're teaching quality, standards-based physical education with the objective of helping young people become active for life.

Have fun with adventure racing CORE, and always remember that student learning is the focus. It's when learning is fun that students accomplish the most.

References

Burnett, M. 2001. *Dare to succeed*. New York: Hyperion.

Corbin, C. 2002. Physical activity for everyone: What every physical educator should know about promoting physical activity. *Journal of Teaching Physical Education* 21:128-144.

Corbin, C., and R. Lindsey. 2007. *Fitness for life*. 5th ed. Champaign, IL: Human Kinetics.

Crowhurst, M.E., J.R. Morrow, J.M. Pivarnik, and J.T. Bricker. 1993. Determination of the aerobic benefit of selected physical education activities. *Research Quarterly for Exercise and Sport* 64:223-227.

DeJager, D. 2004. Attitudes and intensity of middle school students in a traditional versus a nontraditional physical education lesson. Unpublished master's thesis, California State University, Sacramento.

Fisher, D., and J. Levine. 1999. Hypothermia for fun and profit. *Forbes* 164(11):474-479.

Hastad, D., and A. Lacy. 1998. *Measurement and evaluation in physical education and exercise science*. 3rd ed. Needham Heights, MA: Allyn & Bacon.

Herman, J., P. Aschbacher, and L. Winters. 1992. *A practical guide to alternative assessment*. Alexandria, VA: Association for Supervision and Curriculum Development.

Himberg, C., G. Hutchinson, and J. Roussell. 2003. *Teaching secondary physical education: Preparing adolescents to be active for life*. Champaign, IL: Human Kinetics.

Le Masurier, G., and C. Corbin. 2006. Top 10 reasons for quality physical education. *Journal of Physical Education, Recreation and Dance* 77(6):44-53.

Middle and Secondary School Physical Education for Children (MASSPEC). 1995. Appropriate practices for middle school physical education. National Association for Sport and Physical Education.

Middle and Secondary School Physical Education for Children (MASSPEC). 1998. Appropriate practices for high school physical education. National Association for Sport and Physical Education.

Murphy, A., and P. McEntegart. 2001. Urban warriors. *Sports Illustrated* 95(9):15-16.

National Association for Sport and Physical Education. 2004. *Moving into the future: National standards for physical education*. 2nd ed. Reston, VA: Author.

National Association for Sport and Physical Education. 2004. *Physical activity for children: A statement of guidelines for children ages 5-12*. 2nd ed. Reston, VA: Author.

Prichard, N. 1995. Funny, you don't look like an adventure athlete. *Women's Sports & Fitness* 17(8):19-20.

Redfield, K. 2003. Brace yourself. *American Fitness* 21(1):19-23.

Regenold, S. 2007. No sleep is part of the ordeal. *New York Times*, May 18.

Sallis, J., B. Simons-Morton, E. Stone, C. Corbin, L. Epstein, N. Faucette, R. Iannotti, J. Killen, R. Klesges, C. Petray, T. Rowland, and W. Taylor. 1992. Determinants of physical activity and interventions in youth. *Medicine and Science in Sports and Exercise* 24(6):S248-S257.

Schnirring, L. 2001. Can exercise gadgets motivate patients? *Physician & Sportsmedicine* 29(1):15-19.

Siedentop, D. 1994. *Sport education: Quality PE through positive sport experiences*. Champaign, IL: Human Kinetics.

Sieger, M. 2003. Paddle faster, mom. *Time* 161(18):85.

Taylor, W., S. Blair, S. Cummings, C. Wun, and R. Malina. 1999. Childhood and adolescent physical activity patterns and adult physical activity. *Medicine and Science in Sports and Exercise* 31(1):118-123.

About the Authors

Dan DeJager, MS, is a physical education teacher and new teacher mentor in the San Juan Unified School District in Sacramento, California. Mr. DeJager has coached several sports and has served as a school intramural director. He also has worked on several committees, including the Physical Education Curriculum Framework and Criteria Committee for the California State Department of Education. Mr. DeJager has published an article on adventure racing in the *Journal of Physical Education, Recreation & Dance,* and has made numerous presentations at the state and national levels on adventure racing.

He earned an MS in kinesiology from California State University, Sacramento in 2004.

Cathrine Himberg, PhD, has been teaching physical education teacher education at California State University at Chico since 1996. Every week she spends the equivalent of a school day in the public schools with her university students so that they can get the hands-on experience they need to become effective and reflective teachers. She is the founder and director of CASPER (Center for Advancement of Standards-based Physical Education Reform), an advocacy organization for developmentally appropriate physical education.

She earned an MA in 1992 in exercise physiology from California State University at Chico and a PhD in pedagogy (curriculum and instruction) from Virginia Tech in 1996.